AS/A Level

Meas
for Me

WILLIAM SHAKESPEARE

Oxford
Literature
Companions

Notes and activities: Annie Fox
Series consultant: Peter Buckroyd

OXFORD

UNIVERSITY PRESS

Contents

Introduction

What are Oxford Literature Companions?

Oxford Literature Companions is a series designed to provide you with comprehensive support for popular set texts. You can use the Companion alongside your play, using relevant sections during your studies or using the book as a whole for revision.

Each Companion includes detailed guidance and practical activities on:

- **Plot and Structure**
- **Context**
- **Genre**
- **Characterization and Roles**
- **Language**
- **Themes**
- **Performance**
- **Critical Views**
- **Skills and Practice**

How does this book help with exam preparation?

As well as providing guidance on key areas of the play, throughout this book you will also find 'Upgrade' features. These are tips to help with your exam preparation and performance.

In addition, in the extensive **Skills and Practice** chapter, the 'Exam skills' section provides detailed guidance on areas such as how to prepare for the exam, understanding the question, planning your response and hints for what to do (or not do) in the exam.

In the **Skills and Practice** chapter there is also a bank of **Sample questions** and **Sample answers**. The **Sample answers** are marked and include annotations and a summative comment.

How does this book help with terminology?

Throughout the book, key terms are **highlighted** in the text and explained on the same page. There is also a detailed **Glossary** at the end of the book that explains, in the context of the play, all the relevant literary terms highlighted in this book.

Which edition of the play has this book used?

Quotations and character names have been taken from the Oxford School Shakespeare edition of *Measure for Measure* (ISBN 978-019-839335-1).

How does this book work?

Each book in the Oxford Literature Companions series follows the same approach and includes the following features:

- **Key quotations** from the play
- **Key terms** explained on the page and linked to a complete glossary at the end of the book
- **Activity boxes** to help improve your understanding of the text
- **Upgrade** tips to help prepare you for your assessment

Activity boxes to help improve your understanding of the play

Key quotations from the play

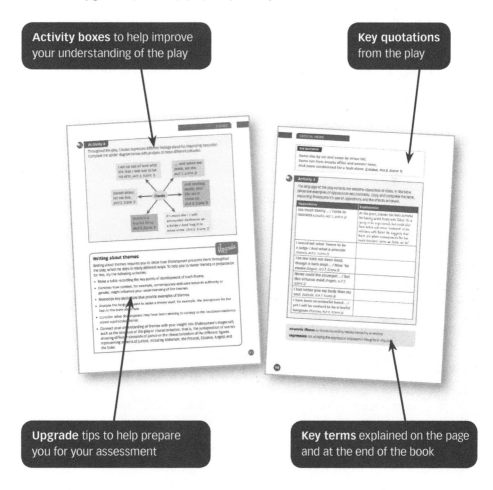

Upgrade tips to help prepare you for your assessment

Key terms explained on the page and at the end of the book

Plot

Measure for Measure (1603–04), a late **comedy** by William Shakespeare, is set in Vienna and explores ideas about power, justice, sex and religion.

Act 1, Scene 1

Vincentio, the Duke of Vienna, tells his counsellor Escalus that he is going away and appointing Angelo who is perceived as a virtuous man, to rule the city in his absence. When Angelo arrives, the Duke explains to him that he will now be in control of the government: **'Mortality and mercy in Vienna / Live in thy tongue and heart'**.

Act 1, Scene 2

On a street in Vienna, Lucio, a comic character and friend to Claudio, learns from the brothel keeper Mistress Overdone that Claudio has been sentenced to death by Angelo for getting his lover Juliet pregnant. Pompey, a tapster (someone who serves alcoholic drinks in a tavern or taphouse) and a pimp, gossips about some of Angelo's other initiatives, such as destroying brothels: **'All houses in the suburbs of Vienna must be plucked down'**. Claudio appears, escorted by the Provost and others, on his way to prison. Claudio tells Lucio to find his sister at the convent and ask her to beg Angelo to spare his life.

> **Key quotation**
>
> When she will play with reason and discourse,
> And well she can persuade.
> *(Claudio)*

comedy a play that ends happily for most of the characters and often focuses on amusing characters or incidents

The Duke believes he is leaving Vienna in Angelo's capable hands

Act 1, Scene 3

At the friary, the Duke explains to Friar Thomas that he feels he may have given the people of Vienna too much 'scope' during the 14 years he has ruled. He thinks he has allowed laws and statutes to 'slip'. The Duke plans to disguise himself as a friar to observe how the 'precise' Angelo delivers justice.

> **Key quotation**
>
> I have deliver'd to Lord Angelo,
> A man of stricture and firm abstinence,
> My absolute power and place here in Vienna
> *(Duke)*

Act 1, Scene 4

Claudio's sister Isabella discusses with a Nun the rules of the convent she has recently entered. The nuns are not allowed to speak to men but, as Isabella is only a novice and 'yet unsworn', she is told to answer the door when Lucio appears. Lucio tells her that her brother Claudio has been sentenced to death because Juliet is 'with child by him'. He asks her to use her powers 'To soften Angelo' and plead for his life. She agrees to try.

> **Key quotation**
>
>   Go to Lord Angelo
> And let him learn to know, when maidens sue
> Men give like gods, but when they weep and kneel
> All their petitions are as freely theirs
> As they themselves would owe them.
> *(Lucio)*

Activity 1

The four scenes of Act 1 occur in four different locations: the Duke's office, a street near a brothel, a friary, and a convent. What is the effect of the action moving suddenly between these different locations from the most powerful seat of government to a street occupied by the underclasses, and then to two religious buildings, one for men and the other women? What do these changes of locations suggest about the concerns and **themes** of the play?

theme subject or idea that is repeated or developed in a literary work

Act 2, Scene 1

In a court room, Angelo tells Escalus that they must enforce the law and that Claudio 'must die'. Escalus recommends caution, asking if Angelo doesn't have faults of his own. Angelo tells the Provost that Claudio is to be executed the next morning. Elbow, a simple constable, presents a case against Pompey, who works with Mistress Overdone, and Froth, who is a client at the taphouse. Angelo leaves in irritation and Escalus hears the case, sending the men off with a warning. Escalus speaks to the Justice about his concerns about the proposed death of Claudio.

Activity 2

In Act 2, Scene 1, Shakespeare shows two sides of justice: the serious judgement against Claudio and the frivolous case against Pompey and Froth. What is the effect of juxtaposing these two different court cases in this scene?

> **Key quotations**
>
> **Whether you had not sometime in your life**
> **Err'd in this point which now you censure him**
> *(Escalus)*
>
> **Some rise by sin and some by virtue fall**
> *(Escalus)*

Act 2, Scene 2

Angelo confirms to the Provost that Claudio is to die tomorrow and tells him not to question him about it again. The Provost asks what should be done with Juliet, who will shortly have her child. Angelo orders that Juliet be taken away and provided with 'needful, but not lavish, means'. A servant announces that Isabella has arrived to speak to Angelo. Isabella and Lucio enter. Isabella pleads, with Lucio's encouragement, for her brother's life. Angelo finally agrees to think about it, asking her to return the next day. Left on his own, Angelo admits in a **soliloquy** that he has been tempted by Isabella and feels guilty about this: 'Dost thou desire her foully for those things / That make her good?'.

> **soliloquy** when characters are left alone on stage (or believe they are alone) and speak their private thoughts aloud

> **Key quotation**
>
> **The law hath not been dead, though it hath slept.**
> *(Angelo)*

Activity 3

This scene is a turning point in the audience's understanding of Angelo, who displays a vulnerability that is surprising given the severity of his actions and his reputation. Identify where in the scene his attitude towards Isabella changes. How does Shakespeare show this change? Make notes on how an actor might portray these changes.

Act 2, Scene 3

The Duke, disguised as a friar, and the Provost speak to Juliet in prison. The Duke discusses Juliet's 'sin' with her and tells her that Claudio is due to be executed the next day.

> **Key quotations**
>
> **Then was your sin of heavier kind than his.**
> (Duke)
>
> **I do repent me as it is an evil**
> **And take the shame with joy.**
> (Juliet)

Act 2, Scene 4

As ordered, Isabella returns to Angelo's office. He says that her brother must die, though he could live longer if she would 'lay down the treasures' of her body. Isabella says that her brother must die because she would be doomed to 'die for ever' if she was to give herself to Angelo. He argues and pleads with her, declaring that he loves her. Isabella threatens to 'tell the world' what Angelo is really like if he doesn't pardon her brother, but Angelo says no one will believe her word against his. After Angelo leaves, Isabella resolves not to give in to him.

> **Key quotations**
>
> **We are all frail.**
> (Angelo)
>
> **Say what you can, my false o'erweighs your true.**
> (Angelo)
>
> **Then Isabel live chaste, and brother die:**
> **More than our brother is our chastity.**
> (Isabella)

Activity 4

a) Both Act 2, Scene 2 and Act 2, Scene 4 end with soliloquies. In one, Angelo reveals his most private thoughts about Isabella, while in the second, Isabella declares her determination to resist him. Compare and contrast what we learn about these two adversaries in these soliloquies.

b) Act 2, Scene 4 is one of the most famous and shocking scenes in the play. As you read it, think about how it could be staged to emphasize the changing arguments and attitudes of the characters.

Act 3, Scene 1

In the prison, the Duke, still disguised as a friar, counsels Claudio. Isabella arrives and tells Claudio what Angelo has proposed, while the Duke and Provost secretly listen. Isabella explains that if it were 'but my life' she would give it up for Claudio's 'deliverance' but that she cannot commit this sin. Claudio tries to argue that it is 'the least' of the seven deadly sins and that 'Death is a fearful thing'. Isabella reacts angrily to Claudio's suggestion that she commit a sin in order to 'save a brother's life'. The Duke interrupts them; he claims that he is Angelo's confessor and that Angelo never meant to 'corrupt' Isabella but was just testing her. The Duke tells Isabella about Mariana, who was engaged to Angelo, but how Angelo left her when her brother died at sea and could no longer provide a dowry for her. He suggests that Isabella agrees to meet with Angelo but that they substitute Mariana in her place.

Tips for assessment

As you read a play, notice when the mood changes, as it frequently does in *Measure for Measure*. How is the mood in the scene between Claudio and Isabella altered by the entrance of the Duke?

Activity 5

a) In this scene, the audience learns about some of Angelo's previous actions. Make a bullet point list of what he has done and analyse if this might change how the audience feels about him as a character in comparison to the original descriptions of him.

b) In this scene, the Duke's role seems to change from observer to active participant and manipulator. Why do you think he has decided to take a more active role?

> ### Key quotations
>
> Dost thou think, Claudio,
> If I would yield him my virginity
> Thou might'st be freed!
> *(Isabella)*
>
> Sweet sister, let me live.
> *(Claudio)*
>
> The hand that hath made you fair hath made you good
> *(Duke)*

Act 3, Scene 2

Still at the prison, the Duke encounters Elbow, who describes the imprisoned Pompey's crimes. Lucio arrives but refuses to put up bail for Pompey. Lucio asks the 'friar' for any news of the Duke. Lucio describes how cold and ruthless Angelo is, and then goes on to gossip about the Duke: **'A very superficial, ignorant, unweighing fellow'**. He claims to know the Duke very well and the 'friar' says that if the Duke ever returns **'let me desire you to make your answer before him'**.

> ### Key quotations
>
> It was a mad fantastical trick of him to steal from the state and usurp the beggary he was never born to.
> *(Lucio)*
>
> He shall know you better, sir, if I may live to report you.
> *(Duke)*

Activity 6

Shakespeare used the device of a powerful character who, while in disguise, learns the uncensored thoughts of other characters in other plays. For example, in *Henry V,* Act 4, Scene 1, King Henry wanders in disguise among his soldiers, discovering their attitudes towards him and their fears about the upcoming battle. In this scene from *Measure for Measure,* what does the Duke learn about Lucio's attitude towards him and how is comedy created by Lucio's being unaware of the Duke's identity?

Act 4, Scene 1

The Duke, still disguised as a friar, meets Mariana, the woman who was formerly betrothed to Angelo. The Duke tells her that he may have some news that will be of 'some advantage' to her. Isabella arrives and explains that she has agreed to meet Angelo in the middle of the night and that she has been given a key to let herself in through the garden gate. The Duke has Isabella explain the plan to Mariana, to which Mariana agrees. The Duke assures Marianna that as Angelo is her husband by a 'pre-contract' she will not be committing a sin.

Activity 7

Why do you think the audience does not hear the two women discussing the Duke's plan? What could have been the reasons why Shakespeare did not provide **dialogue** for this?

Act 4, Scene 2

The Provost asks Pompey to assist the executioner Abhorson. Pompey questions Abhorson and then agrees. The Provost calls for the prisoners Barnardine and Claudio, but only Claudio comes. The murderer Barnadine is sleeping and 'will not wake'. The Provost tells Claudio to prepare himself for his execution, but hopes that there will be 'some pardon or reprieve'. The 'friar' arrives and asks the Provost if there has been a 'countermand' yet for Claudio. A messenger arrives and the Duke assumes this will be Claudio's pardon. However, instead it is a letter from Angelo demanding not only Claudio's execution but that his head be brought to him 'by five'. The Duke plots with the Provost to have Barnardine executed in Claudio's place and his head brought to Angelo. He convinces the Provost by showing him 'the hand and seal of the duke' and explains that the Duke will arrive within two days.

> **Key quotations**
>
> When vice makes mercy, mercy's so extended
> That for the fault's love is th'offender friended.
> *(Duke)*
>
> Call your executioner, and off with Barnardine's head.
> *(Duke)*

Activity 8

How does Shakespeare build **tension** and **suspense** in relation to Claudio's upcoming execution?

Act 4, Scene 3

Pompey compares the inhabitants of the prison with the customers of the brothel, describing their many faults and crimes. Abhorson asks that Barnardine be brought forward for execution. Barnardine refuses as he says he has been drinking all night and is **'not fitted for't'**. The Duke arrives and eventually agrees that Barnardine is **'Unfit to live or die'** and sends him back to his cell. The Provost says that they have another prisoner, Ragozine, who died that morning of a fever. As that prisoner looks like Claudio, they will send his head to Angelo instead. Isabella arrives to ask if Claudio has been pardoned. The 'friar' tells her that her brother was executed. Isabella is distressed, but the 'friar' promises her revenge. Lucio arrives and says that the **'old fantastical duke'** would have spared Claudio's life. Lucio claims that he knew the Duke well and that he was a woman-chaser.

Tips for assessment

Never simply retell the story of the play but instead analyse why events occur in a certain order or what particular effects are achieved by introducing a character at a particular point. For example, why do you think Barnardine is introduced at this late point in the play?

> **Key quotation**
>
> Unhappy Claudio, wretched Isabel,
> Injurious world, most damned Angelo!
> *(Isabella)*

Activity 9

In this scene there are several incidences of **dramatic irony**. The audience is aware that the 'friar' is really the Duke, although various other characters onstage are not. The audience knows that Claudio has not been executed, but Isabella does not. The audience knows that Lucio is insulting the Duke to his face, though Lucio does not. Write a paragraph describing the effect of the use of dramatic irony in this scene.

dialogue conversation between two or more characters

dramatic irony when the audience knows something one or more characters on stage do not

suspense intense emotion while awaiting the outcome of an event

tension increased anxiety, fear or stress

Act 4, Scene 4

Angelo and Escalus discuss the letters they have received from the Duke. They have been asked to meet the Duke at the city's gate and they make arrangements to greet him there. Left alone, Angelo expresses guilt at what he supposes was the deflowering of Isabella and the execution of Claudio.

> **Key quotation**
>
> Alack, when once our grace we have forgot,
> Nothing goes right: we would, and we would not.
> *(Angelo)*

Act 4, Scene 5

The Duke returns, dressed in his usual clothes, and makes plans with Friar Peter to assemble people at the gate.

Act 4, Scene 6

At Mariana's house, Isabella and Mariana discuss the Duke's plan, which involves Isabella accusing Angelo of forcing her to have sex with him. Friar Peter announces that the Duke is arriving at the gates.

Act 5, Scene 1

At the city's gates, the Duke is greeted by Angelo and Escalus. The Duke thanks Angelo for his service. Friar Peter enters with Isabella, who kneels and accuses Angelo of persuading her to give the 'gift' of her 'chaste body' in order to free her brother. However, she has discovered that he did not honour his bargain. The Duke defends Angelo and says he wonders if Isabella is suffering from an 'infirmity of sense'. Friar Peter says that she will be 'disproved'. Mariana enters wearing a veil and accuses her 'husband' Angelo. She reveals her face. Angelo dismisses Mariana's claim. She says that on Tuesday night Angelo 'knew me as a wife'. The mysterious 'friar' is sent for and the Duke exits only to shortly return disguised again as the friar. Lucio insults the 'friar', accusing him of having said negative things about the Duke. The Provost goes to arrest the 'friar'. The Duke stops him and reveals his true identity. Angelo immediately admits his guilt: 'I should be guiltier than my guiltiness'. The Duke orders Mariana and Angelo to be married immediately. The Duke then sentences Angelo to death at 'the very block / Where Claudio stoop'd to death'. Mariana and Isabella beg for Angelo's life, whom the Duke duly spares. The Duke orders for Barnardine to be brought in but instead Claudio enters, to the surprise of all who thought he had been executed.

The Duke promises to punish Lucio and declares that Lucio must marry the woman who claimed he had 'begot' her with child. The Duke unites Juliet with Claudio and Mariana with Angelo. The Duke ends the play by proposing to Isabella.

Isabella accuses Angelo of having deceived her

> **Key quotation**
>
> Whereto, if you'll a willing ear incline,
> What's mine is yours, and what is yours is mine. *(Duke)*

Activity 10

Act 5 is unusual, when compared to the other acts, in that it contains only one scene.

a) Make a bullet point list of the key plot points that occur in this scene.

b) What dramatic effect is achieved by having all the different strands of the plot in this single scene?

c) In J.W. Lever's introduction to the Arden edition of *Measure for Measure*, he argues that the play has three key plots, which would be familiar to Elizabethan audiences. He describes them as:

- 'The Corrupt Magistrate', which is the plot involving Angelo's proposal to Isabella

- 'The Disguised Ruler,' which involves the Duke's adventures while he is in disguise, including his conversations with Lucio

- 'The Substituted Bedmate' (known in earlier plays as 'the bed trick'), which is the plan to substitute Mariana for Isabella.

As you read the play, note when each of these plots is **foregrounded** and consider how they are all resolved in the final act.

---

foregrounded brought to prominence / to the attention of the audience

Structure

It is thought that, in Shakespeare's time, plays were played straight through without interval, unless they were performed in an indoor space using candlelight, when there may have been breaks to replace the candles. Although there are no existing full manuscripts of Shakespeare's plays in his own writing, it is believed that they were originally written without divisions into acts. The acts and scenes were inserted by subsequent editors of the plays when they were published. The editors used the five-act structure, with each act being further divided into scenes. Broadly speaking, an act indicates a unit of the action of the plot, while scenes can indicate a change of location, the entrance or exit of characters, or a passage of time.

Five-act structure

The five-act structure was introduced in ancient Roman times and was the most popular dramatic structure until the 18th century; modern plays more often adhere to a two- or three-act structure. Gustav Freytag, a 19th-century German writer, famously analysed the structure of five-act plays by breaking them down into the following components:

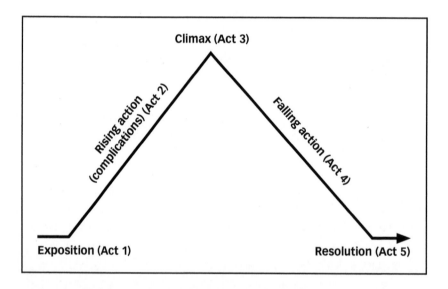

This is a useful way to begin analysing the different elements of the structure, but you may disagree with Freytag's analysis. For example, you may feel that the climax of the play occurs in Act 4 rather than Act 3, or that complications are introduced throughout the text. As a man of the theatre, Shakespeare would have been aware that a version of the five-act shaping of the tale would be expected by his audience, so would mould his plot to include the introduction of a problem, increasing tension and a final resolution.

Activity 11

Using a table like the one below, analyse the structure of *Measure for Measure*. Some details have been added for you.

Structural function	Explanation
Exposition: Setting and characters are introduced and background information is supplied. Possible future actions and conflict are suggested.	Act 1, Scene 1: • Main characters like the Duke and Angelo are introduced. • The Duke's plan to hand his authority over to Angelo is explained. Future actions are suggested as a consequence of giving Angelo power. Act 1, Scene 2: • Characters from the underclasses are introduced, contrasting with the 'court' characters. • Angelo's actions are beginning to be felt. • Claudio's arrest suggests future conflict.
Complications: Problems and conflicts occur. Events begin to speed up.	Act 2, Scene 2: • Complication: Angelo finds himself attracted to Isabella. Isabella is a novice nun and resolved to remain chaste. Act 2, Scene 4: • Complication: Angelo offers a 'deal' to Isabella to save her brother.
Climax: The conflict reaches its tensest point. There may be a turning point that affects the outcome of the play.	Act 4, Scene 2: • Tension builds as the Provost and Duke wait to learn if Angelo will offer a reprieve for Claudio.
Falling action: The events after the plot's climax, which eventually lead to the resolution.	
Resolution: The conflict is resolved and, as a comedy, there is a happy ending. (Tragedies end unhappily, often with the death of the main character.)	

Plot and sub-plot

The main plot of the play centres on Angelo's demand that Isabella surrenders her virginity in order to save her brother's life. The key points in this plot are:

- Act 1, Scene 1: Angelo and his new authority are introduced.
- Act 1, Scene 2: Claudio is arrested and asks Lucio to tell his sister Isabella to plead on his behalf.
- Act 2, Scene 2: Isabella pleads with Angelo. Angelo is attracted to her and asks her to return the next day.
- Act 2, Scene 4: Angelo offers to pardon Claudio in exchange for Isabella's virginity.
- Act 3, Scene 1: Isabella tells Claudio of Angelo's request. Claudio says he wants to live. The Duke devises his plan to substitute Mariana for Isabella.
- Act 4, Scene 2: Despite believing Isabella surrendered, Angelo doesn't pardon Claudio.
- Act 5, Scene 1: The Duke reveals Angelo's crimes and settles scores.

Alongside this main plot, there are the **sub-plots** involving the comic characters of Pompey, Mistress Overdone, Elbow and Lucio. Of these, only Lucio significantly influences the main plot as he is Claudio's friend and urges Isabella to plead with Angelo on her brother's behalf. However, these characters echo themes of the play such as justice, sexual desire and corruption.

Activity 12

a) Use a chart like the one below to note the key points of the main plot in one colour. Then, in another colour, add the key points of the sub-plot, such as the trial of Pompey and Froth in Act 2 or Lucio insulting the Duke in Act 4.

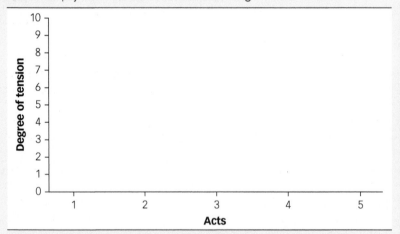

b) Write a paragraph explaining how the sub-plots involving the comic characters reinforce the themes of the play. For example, how is Escalus's judgement about Froth different from Angelo's judgement of Claudio?

Handling of time

Much has been written about Shakespeare's inconsistent handling of time in this play. Critics disagree about how many days are represented, with some suggesting that the whole action takes place over only three days, while others believe it depicts a longer time span. One view is that only a few hours pass between Act 1, Scene 1 and Act 1, Scene 2, whereas others feel that, even with super-human effort, Angelo could not have arranged for the pulling down of the 'houses of resort in the suburbs' *(Act 1, Scene 2)* and Claudio's arrest so quickly. In Act 3, Scene 2, Lucio guesses that the Duke may be 'with the Emperor of Russia' or in Rome, very distant places for a 17th-century traveller to reach in a day or two. There is also the matter of Claudio's shifting execution time and date. On different days, his execution is said to be scheduled for 'tomorrow'. The time of execution is variously given as: 'by nine tomorrow morning' *(Act 2, Scene 1)*; 'provide your block and your axe tomorrow, four a clock' *(Act 4, Scene 2)*; only a few lines later 'by eight tomorrow / Thou must be made immortal' *(Act 4, Scene 2)*, with Angelo's letter later in the same scene setting it again for four o'clock.

Throughout the play, specific times of day and dates are mentioned, emphasizing the importance of the passing of time. Mariana, for example, is very clear that 'But Tuesday night last gone, in's garden-house, / He knew me as a wife' *(Act 5, Scene 1)*. In Act 4, Scene 2, the Duke, disguised as the friar, asks the Provost for 'four days' respite' in the execution of Claudio and later in the same scene assures the Provost that the duke will return 'within these two days' *(Act 4, Scene 2)*. The audience is constantly reminded of the passing of time and approaching events, without these timings being entirely consistent.

There are different interpretations for Shakespeare's handling of time in this play. One is that he developed two different time schemes for the play, one in which the urgency and threat of Claudio's execution are important, while the comic characters occupy a different time scale. Another is that he was writing for a theatre audience rather than for a readership so his primary concern was that his audience felt the same subjective anxiety that Isabella and Claudio do. He persistently reminds them of the terrible consequences of delay, with any variations of timing probably being accepted unquestioningly by the audience, who would be caught up in the action. It is also possible that they are simply errors that occurred either in the writing of the play or when it was transcribed or printed. As this play combines a mixture of tragedy and comedy, this handling of time creates different effects. The breakneck speed of some scenes adds to the comedy and absurdity of them. The compression of time in the main plot contributes to the sense of impending doom, with the threat of Claudio's death and the question of Isabella's sacrifice hanging over the play's action. In the final act, Lucio's persistent interruptions comically slow down the plot as it is hurtling towards its conclusion.

sub-plot a secondary, less important plot

Once Claudio is sentenced to death and Angelo makes clear that he wants the execution to take place quickly, the whole play speeds up as if to test Isabella's and the Duke's ability to save Claudio's life.

Activity 13

Act 4, Scene 2 is an interesting one to study for its handling of time. It occurs at night and involves a number of different characters as they await news of the next day's execution. Read the scene carefully and then answer the following questions.

a) How many times is the word 'tomorrow' said in this scene and what is the effect of the repetition of this word?

b) What words and phrases show that this scene is taking place at night with morning approaching?

c) Does the dialogue between Abhorson and Pompey indicate that they feel the same urgency as the other characters?

d) In your opinion, should sections of this scene be performed more quickly than others? What do you think the **pace** and **rhythm** of the scene should be?

e) How and where does Shakespeare increase and decrease the tension throughout the scene?

---

pace how quickly or slowly something is performed

protagonist the central character, who must overcome obstacles in an attempt to achieve a goal

rhythm the timing and speed of a scene, such as exchanges of dialogue that are slow and steady or quick and erratic

Introduction of characters

One way in which a playwright can shape the structure of a play is to decide when and how characters are introduced. In the first scene of *Measure for Measure*, the Duke and Escalus prepare the audience for Angelo's entrance. They both describe Angelo positively: the Duke has 'dress'd him with our love' and Escalus concurs that Angelo is worthy of 'ample grace and honour' *(Act 1, Scene 1)*. Our expectations of Angelo are therefore high before he has even appeared. As the play develops, this initial opinion of Angelo is contradicted by his dishonourable actions. His downfall is more powerful because he has first been raised in the audience's esteem.

Act 4 sees the first appearances of several notable characters such as Mariana (Scene 1), Abhorson (Scene 2) and Barnardine (Scene 3). At this late stage, many plays are focused on the **protagonist's** plight, but Shakespeare uses the delayed introduction of these characters to develop key themes, such as love and justice. The prison scenes briefly reintroduce minor characters like Elbow and Mistress Overdone, further adding to the complexity of the play's comic sub-plots, which are performed in the shadow of Claudio's imminent execution.

Note also that it is the Duke who both starts and ends the play, speaking its first and last lines, emphasizing his dominance over its plot and structure.

Foreshadowing and tension

Foreshadowing is a way of creating anticipation and tension in the audience. The title of the play is the first example of foreshadowing as the audience expects that at least one character will be judged (measured) as harshly as they judged another, which is Angelo's fate.

Angelo's Act 2, Scene 2 soliloquy foreshadows his actions towards Isabella when he expresses his desire to 'raze the sanctuary / And pitch our evils there', which he then makes explicit in Act 2, Scene 4. The Duke's eventual proposal of marriage to Isabella is foreshadowed by his line in Act 3, Scene 1: 'The hand that hath made you fair hath made you good'.

Shakespeare also creates anticipation and tension by explicitly stating when the next scenes of confrontation will occur. At the end of Act 2, Scene 2, Angelo orders Isabella to 'Come again tomorrow', creating anticipation of their next debate. After their Act 2, Scene 4 encounter, Isabella announces she will tell Claudio 'of Angelo's request', sure that his 'mind of honour' will cause him to agree with her. This creates tension when, in Act 3, Scene 1, Claudio instead begs for his life.

Writing about plot and structure

Use the checklist below to develop your own writing about plot and structure.

- Have you analysed the plot rather than just retelling it?
- Have you used correct terminology such as 'sub-plot', 'juxtaposition' and 'exposition'?
- Have you considered where and when scenes occur and the time that passes between scenes?
- Have you discussed when, how and why characters are introduced?
- Can you analyse the order of the scenes and the effects created by the juxtaposition of one scene with another?
- Can you identify when the climax and resolution of the play occur?
- Have you considered how Shakespeare creates effects such as tension or comedy through his construction of the plot and structuring of the scenes?

Biography of William Shakespeare

Shakespeare was a poet, playwright and actor, known for writing some of the most powerful and influential plays of all time. Much of his life is a mystery and scholars disagree on details, including his exact date of birth, the number or precise chronology of his plays and his personal beliefs. Below are key points of what is known about his life.

No verified portrait of Shakespeare exists, but the 'Chandos portrait' is one of the most famous contenders

- Shakespeare's parents John Shakespeare and Mary Arden married in 1557.
- William Shakespeare was born and baptized in Stratford-upon-Avon in 1564.
- In 1570, his father, a glove-maker, became the Chief Alderman of Stratford-upon-Avon.
- William studied at a school in Stratford-upon-Avon, learning subjects including Latin, **rhetoric** and literature, probably until the age of 15.
- In 1582, at the age of 18, he married Anne Hathaway. They had three children: Susanna (1583) and twins Judith and Hamnet (1585).
- By the early 1590s, Shakespeare moved to London and began to make a reputation for himself as an actor, playwright and poet.
- The acting company the Lord Chamberlain's Men was established in 1594, with Shakespeare as one of the shareholders.
- Between 1594 and 1598, it is believed he wrote a number of his early plays, including the comedies *The Comedy of Errors* and *The Taming of the Shrew* and the histories *Richard III* and the *Henry VI* trilogy.
- In 1596, his only son Hamnet died.
- Between 1595 and 1599, some of his best-loved comedies like *A Midsummer Night's Dream* and *Much Ado About Nothing* were composed, as was the tragedy *Romeo and Juliet*.
- In 1599, the Globe Theatre was built and was home to the Lord Chamberlain's Men's performances.
- Between 1599 and 1606, Shakespeare's great quartet of tragedies was written: *Hamlet*, *Othello*, *King Lear* and *Macbeth*.
- In 1603–04, *Measure for Measure,* considered to be his final comedy, was written.
- In 1603, Elizabeth I died and James I became king of England.
- The Lord Chamberlain's Men gained the **patronage** of King James and the company was renamed the King's Men.

- Shakespeare's late period writing included *The Winter's Tale* (1609–11) and *The Tempest* (1610–11).
- Shakespeare died in 1616 and was buried in Stratford-upon-Avon.

> **patronage** financial support and encouragement from an influential person
>
> **rhetoric** the art of debate and persuasion

Shakespeare and his contemporaries in the theatre

 … for there is an upstart Crow, beautified with our feathers, that with his Tygers hart wrapt in a Players Hyde, supposes he is as well able to bombast out a blanke verse as the best of you: and being an absolute Johannes factotum, is in his owne conceit the onely Shakes-scene in a countrey.

(Robert Greene, 'Groats-Worth of Wit')

Robert Greene, a Cambridge University-educated Elizabethan author, wrote the above criticism of Shakespeare, who was experiencing his first successes as a writer. The 'Players Hyde' refers to Shakespeare's work as an actor ('player' being an Elizabethan term for actor) and 'beautified with our feathers' suggests that he believes Shakespeare may have been borrowing from other writers or pretending to be someone he wasn't. The derisive phrase 'Johannes factotum' means 'Johnny-do-it-all' and is an equivalent to the modern phrase 'Jack of all trades, master of none'. The tone of the complaint makes clear that Shakespeare's confidence ('upstart') and talent ('bombast out a blanke verse') were attracting attention and that this was all the more surprising because of his relatively humble background. Stephen Greenblatt, the literary historian, believes that Greene, who was a leader of a group of university wits, objected to an unknown actor from the country taking London by storm. Shakespeare may have offered his response in his portrayal of the dissolute knight Falstaff in *Henry IV*, who Greenblatt believes was modelled upon the heavy-drinking, brothel-frequenting Greene.

Unlike contemporaries of Shakespeare's, such as the playwrights Christopher Marlowe (1564–93) or Thomas Middleton (1580–1627), there is no evidence that Shakespeare attended university. Nor did he come from a family with theatrical connections, as did the leading actor of his company Richard Burbage (1568–1619). Instead, he seems to have worked his way up in the London theatrical scene as an actor, while developing his skill as a writer. His early education at the King's New School in Stratford-upon-Avon would have provided the basis of his understanding of poetry, oratory and rhetoric, upon which his practical experience of the theatre was added.

His unusual background was commented on by contemporary poet and playwright Ben Jonson (1572–1637) in his poem 'To the Memory of My Beloved, the Author, Mr William Shakespeare and What He Hath Left Us' when he remarks that Shakespeare had 'small Latin and less Greek', a reference to his lack of a thorough classical education. However, Jonson goes on to praise Shakespeare as a 'star of poets' who was 'not of an age but for all time!' For the son of a glove-maker, his ascent was astounding.

William Shakespeare and Richard Burbage were among the shareholders of the Lord Chamberlain's Men. The shareholders were responsible for all business and artistic decisions of the company, sharing the profits and debts. Most of Shakespeare's wealth derived from his share of the box office from the group's performances, rather than payment for writing the plays or their subsequent publication. He would be aware that he needed to attract an audience and encourage them to return again and again to the theatre. Richard Burbage was one of the most admired and successful actors of the age, for whom it is believed Shakespeare wrote many leading roles, including the title roles in *Hamlet*, *King Lear* and *Macbeth*.

Theatre was a popular form of entertainment during Elizabethan and Jacobean times, attracting audiences from a broad range of society. However, theatres were also viewed with suspicion by many. Rulers worried that they might provide an environment for fostering discontent; Puritans objected to the impropriety of the action both on and off the stage; others simply feared that they could be a breeding ground for disease. In 1596, all theatres were banned within the city limits of London. They were forced to move across the Thames to less reputable areas like Southwark.

An impression of 16th-century theatre-goers

For part of 1603, around the time *Measure for Measure* was written, the Globe Theatre was closed due to the bubonic plague, which spread through London eventually killing 33,000 people. During times when the theatres were closed, performances might take place in private houses or at court. This is one reason why patronage from aristocrats or royalty was so important to the theatrical companies.

Puritans

The Puritans were a 16th-century Protestant Christian group. The word 'puritan' has come to describe somebody who lives by strict moral codes and is opposed to luxury.

Activity 1

Puritans, who were highly religious, with strict ideas about proper codes of conduct, were known to object to the theatre. *Measure for Measure* is considered by many to be one of Shakespeare's most shocking plays. Make a bullet point list of anything in the play that you believe might have been objectionable to a Puritan.

The historical period

Shakespeare was born six years after the coronation of Queen Elizabeth I in 1558. Her reign, until her death in 1603, was a time of great artistic flowering and relative political stability in England. However, there was anxiety about who would succeed the unmarried and childless queen to the throne. The son of Mary, Queen of Scots James I, who had ruled Scotland as James VI since 1567, ascended to the English throne in March 1603. It was during this period of change, when the country moved from the Tudor royal family to the Stuart, from Elizabethan to Jacobean, that *Measure for Measure* is believed to have been written. It is known that James I took an interest in the theatre and gave Shakespeare's company his patronage. In recognition of this, they changed their name from the Lord Chamberlain's Men to the King's Men.

Some critics have suggested that there is a deliberate connection between James I and Shakespeare's portrayal of the Duke. Shakespeare would not directly present political issues on stage (and in *Measure for Measure* he moved the action away from England to Vienna) but he would often address the concerns of his audience, as well as taking an opportunity to flatter his patron. James I believed in the Divine Right of Kings, which asserts that the king rules directly by the will of God and that only God can dethrone an unjust king. This same sense of absolute authority is present in the Duke, about whom the critic Walter Kerr remarked that at the end of the play, 'Everybody gets what the Duke wants'.

One possible incident that may have inspired Shakespeare in his portrayal of the Duke was an occasion in April 1603 when James I attempted to balance justice with mercy in a trial of some conspirators:

> After a number of executions, James resolved upon a striking and carefully timed display of mercy. On the very morning fixed for the execution of a group of conspirators, a letter with the royal countermand was secretly conveyed to the sheriff. The prisoners were actually brought out to the scaffold, expecting immediate death; taken back without explanation; and at last recalled to hear a speech on the heinousness of treason and the surpassing mercy of the monarch who had pardoned their lives. This time the king's **coup de theatre** was an unqualified success…
>
> (J.W. Lever, 'Introduction', *Measure for Measure*)

coup de theatre a dramatic effect notable for its suddenness or element of surprise

Activity 2

After reading the description of James I's 'act of mercy' above, compare it to the threats of execution and subsequent pardons of Claudio and Angelo in the play.

Many scholars believe that no matter where Shakespeare set his plays, whether in Italy, Athens or an imaginary land, he always wrote about the England he knew. Although he used Vienna as the location for *Measure for Measure,* only selected elements of the setting are utilized, while others are ignored. Rather than Austrian names, the characters mainly have Italian names, as is common in many of Shakespeare's comedies, and other characters, like the simple constable Elbow and the young man-about-town Froth, are recognizable English characters saddled with comic English names. However, by setting the play in Vienna rather than London, Shakespeare avoids the accusation of representing figures from English society on stage. Instead the audience may feel transported to a more exotic location, while at the same time noting similarities with their own lives. Another advantage of the Vienna setting is that it was known to be a walled city (as was London), which could heighten the sense of a hothouse-like, enclosed environment teeming with problems. It also gave Shakespeare the liberty to invent the law demanding death for fornication for which Claudio was being punished, which, despite concerns about morality, did not exist in England.

Activity 3

In the Vienna of the play, the audience sees brothels and prisons side by side with courts and convents. Make bullet point notes on the features of the different geographical locations of the city as presented by Shakespeare.

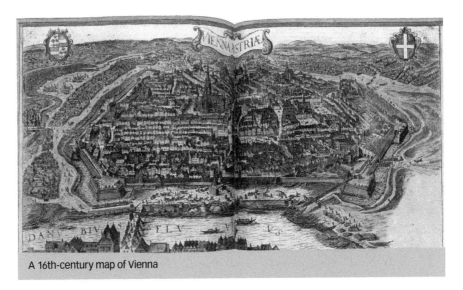

A 16th-century map of Vienna

Religion

 As the only one of Shakespeare's plays to carry a biblical title, *Measure for Measure* draws on an explicitly Christian body of thought about law, mercy, justice, and the right exercise of authority. The pervasive influence of the Sermon on the Mount (Matthew 5–7) over *Measure for Measure's* action has led many critics to interpret the play as a straightforward Christian **allegory** where Mercy pleads before God in a grand Last Judgment.

(Stacy Magedanz, 'Public justice and private mercy in *Measure for Measure*', *Studies in English Literature*)

allegory a story where characters represent moral or political ideas

Some readers misunderstand the title of the play, from Matthew 7, as being simply an 'eye for eye' type exhortation, but it is actually a warning about judging others. The passage begins: 'Do not judge, or you too will be judged. For in the same way you judge others, you will be judged, and with the measure you use, it will be measured to you.' This resonates with Escalus's warnings to Angelo:

> **Key quotation**
>
> Whether you had not sometime in your life
> Err'd in this point which now you censure him
> *(Escalus, Act 2, Scene 1)*

When Isabella is urging Angelo to exercise his mercy, she makes a similar point:

> **Key quotation**
>
> If he had been as you, and you as he,
> You would have slipp'd like him, but he like you
> Would not have been so stern.
> *(Isabella, Act 2, Scene 2)*

Many in Shakespeare's audience would have known the Bible and recognized this passage. The first Bible in English was printed 1525 and further English versions were printed over the subsequent decades, culminating in the King James version, which was completed in 1611. Throughout the play, there are Christian characters and imagery, which encourages the exploration of temptation and mercy.

Henry VIII (1491–1547) was the first ruler of England to impose a state religion and it was during this time that the Church of England (Anglican Church) was founded. The Church of England was formed to allow England to move away from the rule of the Roman Catholic Church (as well as allowing the king to divorce his Catholic wife). Mary I (1516–58) was a Catholic monarch and she actively persecuted Protestants, earning the nickname 'Bloody Mary'. Elizabeth I was a Protestant queen, who appointed Protestants to many key roles; during her reign there was persecution of Catholics, causing many to hide their religious beliefs.

Shakespeare's own religious beliefs are a matter of argument and conjecture among scholars; it has been suggested that his father adhered to Catholic beliefs and some think that Shakespeare may have been brought up Catholic, despite being baptized, married and buried in the Anglican Church. Certainly, he would have found it necessary to present himself as Protestant in accordance with the rulings of both Elizabeth I and her Protestant successor James I. However, Shakespeare frequently located his plays in Catholic countries where he could explore Catholic roles, such as friars and nuns, and traditions such as confession. In *Measure for Measure*, Isabella's plight is highlighted by her commitment to a strict Catholic order which, once she has fully been accepted, will require not only her chastity but her separation from the material world and the company of men. Friars in Shakespeare's plays are often viewed as more worldly characters. For example, it is the Friar in *Romeo and Juliet* who concocts the plan of Juliet's sleeping potion and the Friar in *Much Ado About Nothing* who suggests that they falsely announce Hero is dead while working to clear her reputation. In *Measure for Measure*, Friar Thomas is the only character who is taken into the Duke's confidence and who aids him in his disguise. As a friar, the Duke receives the confidences of a wide range of characters and can frequent places like the prison or Mariana's moated grange without arousing suspicion.

> **Key quotation**
>
> Show me how, good father.
> *(Isabella, Act 3, Scene 1)*

Love and marriage

She should this Angelo have married – was affianced to her oath, and the nuptial appointed; between which time of the contract, and limit of the solemnity, her brother Frederick was wrecked at sea, having in that perished vessel the dowry of his sister.
(Duke, Act 3, Scene 1)

 In late Elizabethan and early Jacobean England, marriage was a long, drawn-out process with a number of steps – from the first private promise of marriage *de futuro* between the two parties themselves, to a public contract and the establishment of property settlement, to the actual church wedding (if that step was even taken at all), and finally, to sexual consummation (if that step had not been taken already).

(Leah Marcus, 'London in *Measure for Measure*', *Shakespeare's Problem Plays*)

Different marital expectations can cause confusion for a modern audience when observing the intricacies of relationships in *Measure for Measure*. At one extreme, you have Isabella and Francisca, who have vowed to remain chaste, and at the other extreme you have the 'Bawd' *(Act 1, Scene 2)* Mistress Overdone who boasts of nine marriages. In between are all the complexities of pre-contracts, private understandings, children born out of wedlock and lost dowries that colour the male/female relationships of the play. What you don't see is an example of a happy marriage.

Claudio and Juliet are charged with the crime of fornication, which is sexual intercourse between two people who are not married. However, given the many stages of marriage and their apparent mutual commitment to each other, this judgement is very harsh. Even the highly religious Isabella's first reaction is 'O, let him marry her' *(Act 1, Scene 4)*, perhaps seeing the problem more as one of unfortunate timing that Juliet has become pregnant rather than the sexual act itself. She must also believe that Mariana is, at least in a sense, 'married' to Angelo, otherwise Mariana's substituting her body for Isabella's would be another sin.

In the 1604 Hampton Court Conference, one of the agreed legal and religious actions was to find ways of revising the definition of a lawful marriage, indicating that this was an important issue of the day.

Anne Hathaway was 26 and pregnant when she wed the 18-year-old William Shakespeare. Their first child Susanna was born six months later. Frequently they lived apart, Shakespeare in London while Anne remained in Stratford, causing some to speculate it was an unhappy marriage.

At this time, it was expected that women would provide a dowry, or a 'marriage portion', which was a financial settlement that could be made up of property, cash or goods. Mariana's tragedy is that her dowry was lost at sea, which seems to have caused Angelo to view their contract as null and void. Neither Mariana nor Juliet is shown to have parents who might oversee the progression of their marriage contracts, so both are left at the mercy of others. While it undoubtedly seems cruel that the Duke announces that Mariana should be married to Angelo only for him to be immediately executed, in practical terms, this would have a financial advantage for Mariana, since as Angelo's widow she would gain his property, making her a more attractive prospect for a new husband.

The 'friar' suggests that Juliet is more guilty in the sin of fornication than Claudio because it is beholden on women to be more chaste

Key quotation

> For his possessions,
> Although by confiscation they are ours,
> We do instate and widow you with all
> To buy you a better husband.
> (Duke, Act 5, Scene 1)

misogynist a person who dislikes or is prejudiced against women

At the core of a coherent social structure as he viewed it lay marriage, which for Shakespeare is no mere comic convention but a crucial and complex ideal. He rejected the stereotype of the passive, sexless, unresponsive female and its inevitable concomitant [co-existing thing], the **misogynist** conviction that all women were whores at heart. Instead he created a series of female characters who were both passionate and pure, who gave their hearts spontaneously into the keeping of the men they loved and remained true to the bargain in the face of tremendous odds.

(Germaine Greer, *Shakespeare: A Very Short Introduction*)

 Activity 4

Read Germaine Greer's response above to the female characters and marriage in Shakespeare's plays and then write a paragraph either agreeing or disagreeing with her point of view in relation to the female characters in *Measure for Measure*.

The underworld

 [The writer J. A.] Sharpe also confirms that the suppression of sexuality was only 'one aspect of a wider desire to achieve a disciplined society. Fornication, like idleness, pilfering, swearing and drunkenness, was one of the distinguishing activities of the disorderly'. Further, the Elizabethan and early Stuart period marked an historical highpoint in an authoritarian preoccupation with the disorderly and their efficient prosecution.

(Jonathan Dollimore, 'Transgression and surveillance in *Measure for Measure*', *Shakespeare's Problem Plays*)

It is common for Shakespeare to present characters from different strata of society, such as the mechanicals in *A Midsummer Night's Dream* or the gravedigger in *Hamlet,* who as simple and honest workmen are portrayed alongside aristocrats and royals. However, the depiction of a criminal underclass is unusual. *Henry IV* shows Mistress Quickly's Boar's Head Tavern which Falstaff, his companions and the prostitute Doll Tearsheet frequent. However, Mistress Quickly attempts to maintain at least the semblance of a respectable reputation. *Measure for Measure,* on the other hand, is notable for its frank depiction of an underclass of bawds, prostitutes, pimps, murderers and drunks. These characters are shown speaking explicitly of their exploits and, eventually, being imprisoned for their misdeeds.

Underworld figures would be familiar to audiences of the Globe Theatre, which, being located in Southwark across the River Thames from the city of London, was outside the strict rules of the city and thus home to many disreputable activities with little fear of arrest of the transgressors. During the latter half of the 16th century, large numbers of people flocked to London, providing customers and victims for the various villains of the area. Robert Greene, the Elizabethan writer who criticized Shakespeare, was also known for his pamphlets in which he exposed the various tricks used by 'coney catchers' (a coney is a tame rabbit and therefore easily caught) in separating the unsuspecting from their money. Gambling dens and public houses were popular. Cut-purses operated on streets or in enclosed places like theatres, robbing people by cutting their money bags from their belts. There were bear- and bull-baiting arenas, bloody and cruel sports where a tethered animal would be attacked by dogs. Many brothels, often painted white for easy identification, were located along the Thames. Although prostitution was technically a crime, it was rarely prosecuted, a situation not unlike that depicted in Vienna under the Duke's reign. Froth could be interpreted as a relative innocent who falls under the influence of unscrupulous 'coney-catchers' like Pompey and Mistress Overdone. In 1604, a crackdown on some of the most outrageous behaviour of 'bawds' began.

Activity 5

a) Read Act 2, Scene 1 from Elbow's entrance until Froth's exit and note what you learn about the activities of Mistress Overdone's 'house'.

b) Look at the quotations below and write an analysis about how they contribute to the impression of the underworld characters in the play:

- **she professes a hot-house; which I think is a very ill house** *(Elbow, Act 2, Scene 1)*

- **if it be not a bawd's house, it is pity of her life, for it is a naughty house** *(Elbow, Act 2, Scene 1)*

- **who, if she had been a woman cardinally given, might have been accused in fornication, adultery, and all uncleanliness there** *(Elbow, Act 2, Scene 1)*

- **I never come into any room in a taphouse, but I am drawn in.** *(Froth, Act 2, Scene 1)*

 Most of the punishments for bawdry or fornication depicted in *Measure for Measure* corresponded to actual practices in Shakespeare's London. The bawd Pompey is threatened with whipping (II.i.235 and IV.ii.11) and the fornicators Claudio and Juliet are exposed to public ridicule (I.ii.110) as part of their punishment. Such offenses were at this time routinely punished by whipping at the cart's tail, being forced to stand in a sheet before a church congregation, and ducking [...] But the fornicator Claudio's final doom of beheading had no real counterpart then and would have been regarded by Shakespeare's audience as a Draconian [extremely harsh] measure.

(Wallace Shugg, *Prostitution in Shakespeare's London*)

Sources

Like other playwrights of the time, Shakespeare frequently borrowed elements of his plays from a variety of sources. Some aspects of the plot, such as a person of high status going disguised or lovers in disguise, can be found in many tales and plays over the ages. However, *Measure for Measure* owes a particular debt to Cinthio's *Gli Hecatommithi* (1565), an Italian collection of tales, which also provided inspiration for *Othello*. This may also have contributed to Shakespeare's decision to use Italian names. Even more influential was a play by George Whetstone entitled *The Historie of Promos and Cassandra* (1578) set in Hungary, which not only shared elements of the same central dilemma as *Measure for Measure* but also some structural features. In this play, the king leaves Lord Promos in charge and Promos propositions Cassandra in order to save the life of her brother Andrugio. A significant difference is that in *The Historie of Promos and Cassandra* there is no switching of women: Cassandra does give herself to Promos. When she tells the king of Promos's actions, he orders that Promos marry Cassandra and then be executed, but Cassandra pleads for his life as she is tied with 'bondes of affection' for her new husband.

Activity 6

Read the following excerpt from *The Historie of Promos and Cassandra* and then explain any similarities you can find with Act 2, Scene 4 of *Measure for Measure*. (The spelling may at first surprise you, but most of the words can be deciphered, though it may help to note that the 'u's are often 'v's in modern English.)

Actus.3. Scena. 2.

Promos: Cassandra in thy brothers halfe, thou hast sayde what may be

And for thy sake, it is, if I doe set Andrugio free:

Short tale to make, thy beauty hath, surprised mee with loue,

That maugre wit, I turne my thoughts, as blynd affections moue.

And quite subdued by Cupids might, needed makes mee sue for grace

To thee Cassandra, which doest holde, my freedom in a lace.

Yeelde to my will, and then command, euen what thou wilt of mee,

Thy brothers life, and all that else, may with liking gree.

(*The Historie of Promos and Cassandra*, Act 3, Scene 2)

Similarities with other Shakespeare plays

Similarities can be drawn between *Measure for Measure* and several of Shakespeare's other plays, such as *Hamlet*. Although one is a tragedy and the other a comedy, both plays portray a dysfunctional government, a love that is more cruel than tender, and a lack of justice. Both Hamlet and Angelo, with corruption swirling around them, reveal their tortured thoughts in soliloquies to the audience. However, Angelo represses his sexual nature in public, presenting himself as pious, whereas Hamlet assumes an amusingly vulgar 'antic disposition' *(Hamlet, Act 1, Scene 5)* as part of his disguise. One interpretation is that both Hamlet's distress at his father's murder and Angelo's sudden infatuation with Isabella manifest themselves as forms of mental illness. In the end, both are redeemed, Hamlet through his taking of action and Angelo by the love of Mariana, who declares:

> **Key quotation**
>
> They say best men are moulded out of faults,
> And for the most become much more the better
> For being a little bad
> *(Mariana, Act 5, Scene 1)*

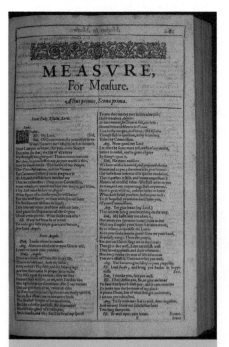

The First Folio's title page for *Measure for Measure*

The presentation of justice and mercy can be compared with that in *The Merchant of Venice*, where Portia delivers her famous speech, 'The quality of mercy is not strained' *(The Merchant of Venice, Act 4, Scene 1)*, as she pleads in court for Shylock to spare Antonio's life. This resonates with Isabella's plea for mercy for Claudio from Angelo, which will 'breathe within your lips / Like man new made' *(Act 2, Scene 2)* as well as Mariana's and Isabella's appeal for clemency for Angelo in the play's final act. Both Portia and Isabella demonstrate extraordinary eloquence and the ability to fashion an impressive argument. At the end of the play, Portia is reunited with her husband Bassanio, while Isabella, despite her vow of chastity, is offered marriage by the Duke. While productions in Shakespeare's age would have depicted these as happy endings, many modern critics find an element of uneasiness in both resolutions, which is often highlighted in 21st-century productions of the plays.

Many aspects of another dark comedy *All's Well That Ends Well* resemble those of *Measure for Measure*. Both have leading male characters – Bertram in the former and Angelo in the latter – who are considered among the least sympathetic of Shakespeare's protagonists and both of whom are tricked in a 'bed-switch' in order to consummate a relationship with a woman he has abandoned. Bertram, who previously rejected his wife Helena, is tricked into sleeping with her by Diana. Both end the play resigned to marriages with women for whom they have expressed little enthusiasm. The Mariana plot line in *Measure for Measure* was an invention of Shakespeare's that was not in the original source material and, although it may be morally more acceptable than the deflowering of Isabella, it does potentially leave Isabella at a loose end at the play's resolution, which may explain the hasty proposal from the Duke. In *Much Ado About Nothing*, Hero is wrongly accused of being a harlot when her waiting woman Margaret, dressed as Hero, and Margaret's lover Borachio are seen in Hero's room as part of a plot to destroy Hero's reputation before her wedding to Claudio. This has potentially tragic consequences for Hero, but the quick actions of an interfering friar save the day, as the Duke does in *Measure for Measure*.

Writing about context

When writing about the context, make sure that you integrate your ideas with your analysis of the play rather than simply bolting on dates and facts. You need to show that your understanding of the context has enriched your insights into the play's themes and characters.

Some aspects of context that you might consider include:

- how religious views of the time may have influenced the writing of the play
- how the rules and traditions about marriage explain the particular dilemmas of characters like Mariana and Juliet
- how the play can be related to other plays by Shakespeare
- how the sources for the story influenced *Measure for Measure*
- how the play's context influences the portrayal of justice and authority in the play
- how concerns about how to deal with disorderly conduct are presented in the play
- how an audience today might perceive aspects of the play differently from an audience in Shakespeare's time.

> The best actors in the world, either for tragedy, comedy, history, pastoral, pastoral-comical, historical-pastoral, tragical-historical, tragical-comical-historical-pastoral, scene individable, or poem unlimited: Seneca cannot be too heavy, nor Plautus too light. For the law of writ and the liberty, these are the only men.
>
> *(Polonius, Hamlet, Act, 2, Scene 2)*

As the above quotation from *Hamlet*, spoken on the arrival of the players to the court in Elsinore, demonstrates, Elizabethan actors performed many different **genres** of drama, including **sub-genres** or **hybrid genres**. *Measure for Measure* is often considered a late comedy but, given its combination of serious themes, raucous humour, cynical tone and unsettling conclusion, it has been categorized in many different ways.

blank verse unrhymed lines of poetry with a regular metre

genre a category or style of literature or art

hybrid genre a work of literature or art that combines elements of two or more different genres

prose any writing in continuous form without rhythm or rhyme; associated with everyday speech

sub-genre a subdivision or more precise genre

tragedy a dramatic genre in which the tragic protagonist experiences a downfall, leading to an unhappy ending

Shakespearean drama

In 1623, the First Folio of Shakespeare's plays was published. This volume contained 36 of Shakespeare's plays, divided into three genres: comedies, tragedies and histories. The First Folio was prepared and edited by John Heminges and Henry Condell, who were actors in Shakespeare's company the King's Men, and both of whom were mentioned in Shakespeare's will. Given their close association with Shakespeare and their personal knowledge of the plays, the First Folio is considered a more reputable version of the plays than some earlier published versions, which may have been pirated, incomplete or corrupted.

However the version of the play you are reading has most likely been edited and corrected further, for example, by adding stage directions or regularizing the characters' names or spellings in order to make the text easier to follow.

In the First Folio, *Measure for Measure* is listed as a comedy, along with 13 other comedies, including *A Midsummer Night's Dream* and *Much Ado About Nothing*, and other plays that are more difficult to categorize like *The Tempest* or *The Winter's Tale*. Also in the volume are 10 histories, such as *Richard III* and *Henry V*; and 12 tragedies, including *Hamlet* and *Macbeth*. The simplicity of the three basic genres is appealing, but even at a glance it raises questions. Shouldn't *Julius Caesar* and *Anthony and Cleopatra* be listed as histories rather than as tragedies? Are *The Tempest*, *All's Well that Ends Well* and *The Winter's Tale* comedies in the same sense as *As You Like It* or *The Comedy of Errors*? Polonius's speech from *Hamlet* indicates that this was an area for discussion in Shakespeare's day (which Shakespeare is likely satirizing by putting these words in the pompous Polonius's mouth). Whatever the specific genre, it is useful to identify certain features of Shakespearean drama.

While it is easy to have a stereotyped image of what Shakespearean performances must have been like, with broad gestures and over-enunciated voices, it is clear from his own writing that Shakespeare was aiming for something more realistic, at least in terms of the style of the day. In Act 3, Scene 2 of *Hamlet*, Hamlet gives advice to the actors which is assumed by many to portray Shakespeare's own advice to actors, including, 'suit the action to the word, the word to the action' and criticizing those who 'strutted and bellowed'. The goal of drama is to hold 'the mirror up to nature', that is, to show the audience the world as it is. By Hamlet's own reaction to the players' acting, it is clear that Shakespeare believes that drama can inform and move the spectator.

Shakespearean dramas are constructed not on the principle of unity of action, but on the principle of analogy, comprising a double, treble, or quadruple plot, which repeats the same basic theme; they are a system of mirrors, as it were, both concave and convex, which reflect, magnify and parody the same situation.

(Jan Kott, *Shakespeare Our Contemporary*)

However, Shakespearean drama is not realistic when compared to modern drama. At the time, **blank verse** and rhymed verse were commonly used and two-thirds of *Measure for Measure* is written in verse, with the rest in **prose**.

Audiences at this time would readily have accepted the use of verse and the switching from verse to prose without question. Similarly, there was an acceptance of mixing comedy with **tragedy**. The critic Jan Kott believes that one of the identifying features of Shakespeare's plays is the way he repeats, distorts and mirrors plots in order to explore an idea. The comic sub-plot of Lucio having impregnated Kate Keepdown mirrors the serious plot of Claudio and Juliet; the comic appointing of Pompey as Abhorson's deputy executioner parodies the serious appointment of Angelo as the Duke's deputy. This layering of plots adds to the richness and complexity of the drama.

Activity 1

Write a bullet point list comparing the depiction of Lucio and Kate Keepdown with that of Claudio and Juliet, including the language used to describe each and the resolution of each plot. In a few sentences, explain how the plots reflect each other and contribute to the overall themes of the play.

Comedy

Laughter is not man's first impulse; he cries first. Comedy always comes second, late, after the fact and in spite of it or because of it.

(Walter Kerr, *Tragedy and Comedy*)

Ancient Greece gave birth to tragedy and comedy. The first comedies often dealt with political issues and satirized well-known figures. They could be very rude, dealing overtly with sex and bodily functions.

The phallus was always onstage in Greek comedy, and the wine-swilling, sexually voracious satyr – an animal-like man and companion of Dionysus [Greek god of fertility, wine and theatre] – is the first of many performers who like to flaunt what they've got…

(Matthew Bevis, *Comedy: A Very Short Introduction*)

It is not a big leap to see satyr-like qualities in a character like Pompey as well as the 'wine-swilling' excesses of Barnardine and the visitors to Mistress Overdone's establishment, like Froth. Some modern productions emphasize the sexual comedy of *Measure for Measure*. In the 2015 Young Vic production directed by Joe Hill-Gibbins, the stage was filled with plastic inflatable sex dolls to exaggerate the sexual preoccupations of the characters. One source of low comedy is the enormous appetite of characters, their almost animalistic urges, whether it is for sex, food or drink, unrepressed by societal expectations. In *Measure for Measure*, the low comedy commonplace in ancient Greek comedy is seen in the underworld scenes and combined with the structure and conventions of Shakespearean comedy.

Although it is common to think that tragedies are plays that make the audience cry and comedies ones that make them laugh, this is far too simplistic. In particular, Shakespearean comedies have certain identifying features that the Elizabethan audience would anticipate and appreciate. Key features include:

- mistaken identities
- witty **wordplay**
- one or more 'clowns' (humorous characters of low status)
- exotic locations
- ending with multiple weddings.

wordplay witty use of words to play upon their multiple or unclear meanings

Activity 2

Use a table like the one below to record examples of the characteristics of Shakespearean comedy that you can locate in *Measure for Measure*. It has been started for you.

Feature	Example from *Measure for Measure*
Mistaken identities	The Duke is disguised as a friar
Witty wordplay	
One or more 'clowns' (humorous characters of low status)	Pompey, Elbow
Exotic locations	
Ending with multiple weddings	

> Shakespeare's comedies are steeped in a rich, diverse heritage of country merriments and holiday customs, including the saturnalia [ancient Roman holiday of over-indulgence and breaking social norms], the carnival, May games, and the election of the Lord of Misrule on Twelfth Night.
>
> (Matthew Bevis, *Comedy: A Very Short Introduction*)

The Lord of Misrule was a figure in medieval England who would mock those in power. Usually associated with Christmas celebrations, the Lord of Misrule was a person of low rank, who would become a lord for the day and command the day's activities. It was a way of turning the social order upside down and mocking authority. In *Measure for Measure* several characters challenge the social order. Lucio insults both the Duke and his alter ego the friar, going so far as to interrupt the Duke's final orders in the play's last act. The prisoner Barnardine is too drunk to be executed. He is the inverse of Claudio, who does not deserve to be executed and who fears death, while Barnardine, a murderer and a prisoner for nine years, is fearless. Yet he disobeys the executioner, turning the rules of the prison upside down, announcing that he **'will not consent to die this day'** as he has been drinking that day so is **'not fitted for't'** *(Act 4, Scene 3)*. In the final act, the Duke forgives Barnardine, despite his indifference to whether he lives or dies.

One of the key elements of a Shakespearean comedy is not only that there should be humour, but that there is a sense of resolution, usually signified by one or more marriages. After the misunderstandings and missed opportunities of the previous acts, marriage represents the return to social order. In a typical Shakespearean comedy, the final image is of assorted couples joined in matrimony.

 In the last scene, when the dramatist usually tries to get all his characters on the stage at once, the audience witnesses the birth of a renewed sense of social integration. In comedy as in life the regular expression of this is a festival, whether a marriage, a dance, or a feast.

(Northrop Frye, 'The Argument of Comedy', *Shakespeare: Modern Essays in Criticism*)

However, it is a matter of interpretation how happy the ending of *Measure for Measure* is. In Shakespeare's time, the ending would probably have been accepted as the correct return to social order, where the newly united characters would finish the play with a dance; modern productions often emphasize the uneasiness of these sudden couplings.

 The ending of *Measure for Measure* (c. 1603–04) pushes things to the limit by getting audiences to think about the suitability of marriage as a symbolic shorthand for comedy's happy-ever-afters. When Mariana enquires of the Duke, 'my most gracious lord, I hope you will not mock me with a husband', she is voicing her fear that she will lose her heart's desire, but the line also glances towards another possibility, for many would consider it a fate worse than death to be married to Angelo. The Duke's final words to Mariana as he marries the couple off ('Joy to you, Mariana') are uttered moments after Angelo himself has admitted: 'I crave death more willingly than mercy'.

(Matthew Bevis, *Comedy: A Very Short Introduction*)

This ambiguity at the end of the play is one of the reasons that scholars question if the play is truly a comedy or if it has been rather forced into the shape of a comedy without fulfilling the light-heartedness associated with the genre.

Problem plays

The term 'problem play' was coined by F.S. Boas in 1896 to describe a selection of Shakespeare's plays that did not easily fall into the genres of tragedy or comedy. In his view, these plays were *Troilus and Cressida, Measure for Measure* and *All's Well That Ends Well*, as well as, more surprisingly, *Hamlet*. At the time, some of the plays produced by Victorian writers were thought of as problem plays, such as those by the realist dramatist Henrik Ibsen. Boas felt that, in a similar way, the four plays by Shakespeare explored moral and social dilemmas, and did not offer easy resolutions. Subsequent critics have removed *Hamlet* from this category, while some have added others, such as *The Winter's Tale*.

In her discussion of problem plays (in *Shakespeare's Problem Plays: Contemporary Critical Essays*), Vivian Thomas identifies several key features, including:

- important scenes of debate
- explorations of the relationship between people and institutions
- the theme of appearance and reality
- portrayal of women as sexual objects.

The critic A.P. Rossiter makes an important point about the problem plays' determined focus on the shortcomings and human foibles of the characters instead of their nobility. The characters frequently express their disillusionment, unhappiness and bitterness. One of the most important qualities of a problem play is a cynical tone, which may cause the audience to question who is the play's protagonist, what is the correct social order and what would constitute a happy ending. While in most comedies or tragedies, it is clear who the heroes or heroines are, in a problem play it may be less obvious.

Activity 3

a) Consider who, in your opinion, is the protagonist of *Measure for Measure*? Whose journey are we following? Is it the Duke, despite his being an observer for much of the play? Is it Angelo or Isabella, despite both having their fates thrust upon them by the Duke rather than having learned and developed throughout the course of the play? At the end of the play, do we feel that the Duke has restored order? Or simply that he has condoned chaos?

b) From your understanding of problem plays, write a paragraph explaining to what extent *Measure for Measure* fits in this genre.

Tragi-comedy

> *Measure for Measure* is tragi-comic in two distinguishable senses. In the first half it moves swiftly towards tragic calamity, twisting deeper and deeper into the quick; then the observer Duke turns ***Deus ex machina***, and the puppet-master makes all dance to a happy ending, with a lot of creaking [...] The other sense in which the play is **tragi-comedy** depends on the parallel running of the same themes in two incongruous tones. The 'tragic' sex-plot of Angelo and Isabella is commingled with the low-life comic stuff, involving Pompey, Mrs Overdone and Lucio, not only in their bawdy or business relations, but also in connection with the operations of summary justice in the underworld.
>
> (A.P. Rossiter, *The Problem Plays in Shakespeare: Modern Essays in Criticism*)

Measure for Measure is often identified as a 'dark comedy' in which grim humour is derived from the bleakest of situations. Act 4 provides examples of this, where the tension of Claudio's upcoming execution is mixed with Barnardine's refusal to be executed and the comic interview between Pompey and Abhorson. These both have a touch of the despair found in the **theatre of the absurd** in which the pointlessness and absurdity of life is comically highlighted. Pompey's cheerful acceptance as he changes jobs from tapster to executioner, and the Duke and Provost's discussion of Barnardine's being 'Unfit to live or die' (*Act 4, Scene 3*), are examples of this dark **gallows humour**.

One of the most serious and dramatic scenes in the play is Act 3, Scene 1 when Isabella explains her rejection of Angelo's proposition to her and Claudio's subsequent appeal that she find a way to help him to live. Despite the grave topic, some productions discover moments of comedy in this scene, highlighting the tragi-comic nature of the play. In the production directed by Simon McBurney at the National Theatre in 2004 (revived in 2006), there were several moments in this scene that provoked laughter from the audience. For example, after Isabella explains that she would lay down her life but not her chastity for Claudio, the actor playing Claudio paused meaningfully between 'Thanks' and 'dear Isabel' indicating that he did not share her conviction.

Deus ex machina a surprising and unlikely plot device that brings about a resolution to what seemed to be an impossible situation

gallows humour humour expressed in a bleak or desperate situation

theatre of the absurd a genre of drama that emerged after the Second World War which ignores many of the conventions of plays, such as conventional plots; it focuses on the hopelessness of man in a meaningless world

tragi-comedy a genre that includes aspects of comedy and tragedy

Activity 4

a) Closely read Act 3, Scene 1 from **'Now, sister, what's the comfort'** to **'Oh hear me, Isabella'**. Identify:

- any moments where the use of pause, gesture or intonation might make a moment comic

- any moments that could be made more tragic by the use of pause, gesture or intonation.

b) Then consider the change in tone and mood in the scene when the Duke enters.

c) Write a paragraph in response to the following question: How does Shakespeare combine the demands of comedy and tragedy in Act 3, Scene 1?

Writing about genre

When writing about the genre of *Measure for Measure*, remember to do the following:

- Write about the play as a play, not as a novel or story.
- Use the correct terminology, such as 'tragi-comedy', 'blank verse' or 'problem play'.
- Notice how scenes or characters could be perceived as being both comic and tragic, or when a scene may shift in tone from light-hearted to dark.
- Be sensitive to the different ways the play may be interpreted.
- Use your understanding of genre to analyse aspects of the play, such as the conventions of comedy or the importance of the play's resolution.

Main characters

Vincentio (the Duke)

The actions of Vincentio, the Duke of Vienna, provide both the catalyst for the plot and its final resolution. He is also the character with the most lines in the play, commanding a surprising 30% of the lines, double those allocated to Isabella and almost three times as many as Angelo. The critic Walter Kerr has compared the Duke to a 'ringmaster' who, with 'a magician's flourish' in Act 5, Scene 1, 'proceeds to put the rabbits into such hats as he thinks proper'. Another view is that he relinquishes his powerful insider status in order, as an outsider, to observe the corrupt world he has ruled. A different view is that he is a holy teacher, who is guiding the characters through a series of tests in order to achieve their ultimate redemption.

However, others have a less sympathetic view of the character. The play begins with the Duke's possibly misguided plan to hand over authority, hoping that Angelo will enforce the law of the land in a different manner from the Duke himself, who has been rather lax for the past 14 years. Instead of shouldering his responsibilities for Vienna, the Duke goes in disguise to spy on his subjects and to observe how Angelo runs the city.

Two of the Duke's scenes, in particular, jar with many modern audiences: Act 2, Scene 3, when he conducts a false confession with the pregnant Juliet, telling her that 'Your partner, as I hear, must die tomorrow' and Act 4, Scene 3, when he bluntly (and falsely) tells Isabella that Claudio has been executed: 'His head is off, and sent to Angelo'. Although it may be that he feels these deceptions are necessary for the final public unmasking of Angelo, their cruelty is striking and audiences may agree with Lucio's description of him as 'the old fantastical duke of dark corners' (Act 4, Scene 3). The wisdom of the Duke's judgement is also called into question both by his choice of Angelo as his deputy at the beginning of the play and his sudden proposal to the novice nun Isabella at the end of the play. Many scholars feel that the Duke is an intriguing but ultimately frustrating character, who provokes a variety of responses from actors and audiences.

The Duke, as portrayed by Ben Miles in Michael Attenborough's 2010 production

Key quotations

Sith 'twas my fault to give the people scope,

'Twould be my tyranny to strike and gall them
(Duke, Act 1, Scene 3)

He who the sword of heaven will bear

Should be as holy, as severe:

Pattern in himself to know,

Grace to stand, and virtue go
(Duke, Act 3, Scene 2)

Vincentio is disreputable: a man of authority, like Theseus [in *A Midsummer Night's Dream*] or Don Pedro [in *Much Ado About Nothing*], who has slid out of his responsibility for the chaos in Vienna to become a meddling false friar.

(David Daniell, 'Shakespeare and the traditions of comedy', *The Cambridge Companion to Shakespeare Studies*)

Activity 1

The actor and writer Simon Callow has described how, in the early 20th century, *Measure for Measure* was not considered very rewarding for actors, describing the Duke as a 'windbag', Isabella 'a prig' and Angelo a 'cold, unattractive figure'. To what extent do you agree with this assessment? Explain your reasons and provide examples from the play.

Angelo

Angelo is a character full of **paradoxes** and contradictions. Even his name is ironic, for he is certainly no angel. He is described by others as **'precise'**, **'strict'** and cold-blooded: **'scarce confesses / That his blood flows'** *(Act 1, Scene 3)* and **'... whose blood / Is very snow-broth'** *(Act 1, Scene 4)*. The Duke feels Angelo's rigidity will be an effective counter to his own laxness. However, rather than expressing confidence in his ability to deputize for the Duke, Angelo hesitates. It could be that he is aware that he does not have the judgement to rule the city or it may be a false show of modesty as, once the Duke leaves, he does not hesitate to put his own stamp on the office. However, there seems to be little logic or justice in his actions.

paradox a statement or situation that seems contradictory or impossible

It might seem reasonable that a character who is often interpreted as a cold Puritan should wish to tear down the bawdy houses, but it is more surprising that the case of Claudio and Juliet has demanded his immediate and severe attention. He appears to prefer justice to be quick and brutal. When the court case involving Elbow and Froth is brought to his attention, he quickly loses patience, commanding Escalus to hear out the case and leaving, saying he hopes Escalus will 'find good cause to whip them all' (Act 2, Scene 1).

His treatment of the pregnant Juliet is unkind: 'Let her have needful, but not lavish, means' (Act 2, Scene 2). However, he agrees to see Isabella when he hears that she is 'shortly of a sisterhood' (Act 2, Scene 2). The difference in his attitude towards Juliet and towards Isabella, before he even meets her, suggests that he divides the world into the good and bad, which, to his mind, these two women represent.

Scholars often point out that Isabella and Angelo are strikingly similar. Both have severe ideas about chastity and the importance of laws. Both are intelligent and capable of nuanced debate. The difference is that Isabella appears to believe what she says, while Angelo is disguising his own desires and capacity for sin. In his soliloquy at the end of Act 2, Scene 2, his surprise at his newly awakened lust seems to alarm him: 'What's this? What's this? Is this her fault, or mine?' (Act 2, Scene 2).

Angelo is arguably the most complex and dramatic role in the play and this role has attracted many leading actors and a wide variety of interpretations. In the 1933 Old Vic production, Charles Laughton played Angelo as a scheming, brooding, black-robed monster. John Gielgud's Angelo, in 1951 at the RSC, had a 'suppressed and twisted nobility'. In the 2010 Almeida Theatre production, Rory Kinnear portrayed Angelo as an awkward, bespectacled, unfashionable pen-pusher.

One of the challenges for the actor playing Angelo is conveying the two sides of his character: the severe, repressed deputy and the man overcome by forbidden desire. For many, it is hard to view Angelo's behaviour in the play sympathetically.

Not only does Angelo make a despicable arrangement with Isabella, he then breaks his side of the bargain, ordering Claudio to be executed despite her apparent submission to him. He has also broken his engagement to Mariana upon the loss of her dowry and sullies her honour by declaring publicly that 'her reputation was disvalued / In levity' (Act 5, Scene 1). He only admits to his wrong-doing towards Isabella when there is absolute proof and then gracelessly marries Mariana. The only defence for him comes from Mariana, who believes he will become 'better / For being a little bad' (Act 5, Scene 1).

Paul Rhys played Angelo as a man tortured by his feelings in the 2004 Complicite/National Theatre production

> **Key quotations**
>
> Lord Angelo is precise,
> Stands at a guard with envy, scarce confesses
> That his blood flows, or that his appetite
> Is more to bread than stone.
> *(Duke, Act 1, Scene 3)*
>
> What, do I love her
> That I desire to hear her speak again
> And feast upon her eyes?
> *(Angelo, Act 2, Scene 2)*

> **Activity 2**
>
> Act 4, Scene 4 shows Angelo in a particularly distressed and distracted state as he believes, falsely as it turns out, that he has deflowered a novice nun and executed her brother. Look at the words or phrases below and explain what they suggest about Angelo's mental state at this point:
>
> - 'unshapes me'
> - 'unpregnant'
> - 'eminent body'
> - 'maiden loss'
> - 'tongue'
> - 'scandal'
> - 'shame'

Isabella

Isabella, along with Angelo and Hamlet, has been described by the critic A.P. Rossiter as one of Shakespeare's 'intellectuals'. The first mention of her is in Act 1, Scene 2 when Claudio asks Lucio to fetch his sister who is in her 'approbation' or trial period at 'the cloister'. He praises her ability to debate and persuade: 'she hath prosperous art / When she will play with reason and discourse, / And well she can persuade' *(Act 1, Scene 2)*. She is not portrayed as a soft, yielding character but rather as someone who shares aspects of Angelo's severity, suggested by her desire that the convent should offer 'a more strict restraint / Upon the sisterhood' *(Act 1, Scene 4)*.

Her name is a variation of 'Elizabeth', which means 'devoted to God'. It was also the name of the former queen of England Elizabeth I, who was known as the Virgin Queen, so if the Duke has aspects of James I (see page 25), there may be some aspects of Elizabeth I in Isabella.

Lucio comments that Isabella is 'Gentle and fair' *(Act 1, Scene 4)* and, in Act 2, Scene 2, the Provost describes her as a 'virtuous maid', but it is her ability with words that seems to captivate. Watched by Lucio and the Provost, Angelo and she conduct a debate on whether the subtleties of Claudio's fault and the law can be analysed so that his life might be saved.

During this scene, Angelo discovers his attraction to Isabella, but she gives no sign of being aware of this. When she says 'Hark how I'll bribe you', Angelo might perceive this as either a financial or sexual bribe, whereas she has innocently suggested a bribe of 'true prayers' *(Act 2, Scene 2)*.

In Act 2, Scene 4, Isabella is presented with the play's central dilemma: should she lay down her virginity in order to save her brother's life? Unlike the source material (Whetstone's play), Shakespeare's heroine refuses the offer. Her reasoning is that she would face eternal damnation: 'Better it were a brother died at once, / Than that a sister by redeeming him / Should die for ever' *(Act 2, Scene 4)*. In her soliloquy at the end of this scene, she confronts the harshness of her position: no one will believe her if she denounces Angelo and she is unwilling to submit to him. She believes that Claudio will support her view, but discovers, in Act 3, Scene 1, that Claudio's perspective is less absolute than hers, causing her further distress until the Duke emerges to take matters in hand. One interpretation is that the Duke discovers his attraction to Isabella upon hearing her passionate speech to her brother.

From the Duke's introduction of his plan, Isabella loses some sense of her ability to act independently to the extent that, at the end of the play, after previously vowing chastity, it is announced that she is to be joined in marriage to the Duke. In the final act, she speaks powerfully in her condemnation of Angelo, but responds to the Duke's proposal with silence.

Key quotations

More than our brother is our chastity.
(Isabella, Act 2, Scene 4)

Is't not a kind of incest to take life
From thine own sister's shame?
(Isabella, Act 3, Scene 1)

   even so may Angelo
In all his dressings, characts, titles, forms,
Be an arch-villain.
(Isabella, Act 5, Scene 1)

Activity 3

At the heart of *Measure for Measure* are three key debates involving Isabella:

- Act 2, Scene 2
- Act 2, Scene 4
- Act 3, Scene 1.

Use a table like the one below to analyse Isabella's character and choice of language in these scenes.

Act and scene	Characters involved	Key arguments	Key quotations
Act 2, Scene 2	Isabella and Angelo (with Lucio and the Provost)		
Act 2, Scene 4	Isabella and Angelo		
Act 3, Scene 1	Isabella and Claudio (overheard by the Duke and the Provost)		

Isabella and Claudio in Act 3, Scene 1 of Simon McBurney's Complicite/National Theatre Revival production, 2006

Claudio

Claudio is Isabella's brother and father to Juliet's baby. He is described in flattering terms by other characters. Mistress Overdone says that Claudio is worth 'five thousand of you all' *(Act 1, Scene 2)* and Escalus argues that Claudio had 'a most noble father' *(Act 2, Scene 1)*.

Claudio's first entrance is in Act 1, Scene 2 when he is being publicly shamed in the streets of Vienna before being taken to prison. He admits he is guilty of 'too much liberty' *(Act 1, Scene 2)*. He agrees that he broke the letter of the law, but not the spirit of it, as he and Juliet were to be married as soon as her dowry was settled.

Claudio and his sister Isabella are very different characters. Claudio lives very much in the world of Vienna. Lucio, an irreverent character who associates with prostitutes, is his close friend and he is at least known to the bawd Mistress Overdone, who praises him. He admits that he and Juliet have enjoyed the 'most mutual entertainment' *(Act 1, Scene 2)*. This contrasts with Isabella, who has retreated to the convent and taken a vow of chastity. Their different characters are demonstrated in Act 3, Scene 1 when, despite her expectations otherwise, Claudio does not whole-heartedly support Isabella's choice of her chastity over his life. His understandable fear of death contrasts with Isabella's certainty that it is better for him to die than for her to commit a sin. Claudio is a man of compromise, arguing that of all the sins, lechery 'is the least' *(Act 3, Scene 1)*.

At the play's end, he is joined in matrimony with Juliet in what may possibly be the only happy marriage in the play.

Activity 4

Claudio's speech in Act 3, Scene 1, which begins 'Ay, but to die and go we know not where...', bears some resemblance to Hamlet's 'To be or not to be' soliloquy. Both are meditations on death and the mysteries of the afterlife. Read the excerpt of the speech from *Hamlet* below and note any similarities with Claudio's speech:

> Who would fardels bear,
> To grunt and sweat under a weary life,
> But that the dread of something after death,
> The undiscovered country, from whose bourn
> No traveller returns, puzzles the will,
> And makes us rather bear those ills we have
> Than fly to others that we know not of?
> Thus conscience does make cowards of us all,
> And thus the native hue of resolution
> Is sicklied o'er with the pale cast of thought,
> And enterprises of great pith and moment
> With this regard their currents turn awry
> And lose the name of action.

(Hamlet, Act 3, Scene 1)

> **Key quotation**
>
> Sweet sister, let me live.
> What sin you do to save a brother's life,
> Nature dispenses with the deed so far
> That it becomes a virtue.
> *(Claudio, Act 3, Scene 1)*

Lucio

Lucio is a character who links the different worlds of the play: the brothel, the convent, the prison and the court. He is Claudio's 'good friend' *(Act 1, Scene 2)* and is one of the comic characters who serves as a guide to the play's underworld. In the play's second scene – a startling contrast to the world of the Duke's court – Lucio, in conversation with two Gentlemen, Mistress Overdone and Pompey, alerts the audience to the excesses of Vienna. In dialogue full of rude **puns** and sexual innuendo, Mistress Overdone's bawdy house and the spread of sexual diseases are discussed. However, once he knows that his friend Claudio is in need, Lucio springs into service. He delivers Claudio's message to Isabella at the convent and convinces her to plead for Claudio's life: 'And that's my pith of business / 'Twixt you and your poor brother' *(Act 1, Scene 4)*.

In Act 2, Scene 2, he accompanies Isabella to Angelo's office and encourages her not to give up: 'Give't not o'er so: to him again, entreat him' *(Act 2, Scene 2)*.

However, Lucio shows himself to be less loyal to his underworld friends. He refuses to put up bail for Pompey and is distraught at the idea of marrying Kate Keepdown, whom he has impregnated. He is also a gossip and a liar, as is evident in his scenes with the Duke. One source of the play's humour is that Lucio, unaware that he is actually speaking to him in disguise, insults the Duke by suggesting that he was a womanizer and a drinker. He goes so far as to declare the Duke a 'very superficial, ignorant, unweighing fellow', which the proud Duke must bear in silence or else reveal his true identity *(Act 3, Scene 2)*. Lucio's name derives from the Latin word 'lux' meaning light and Lucio, either knowingly or unwittingly, has a knack for shedding light on the characters in the play.

pun joke based on different meanings or similar soundings of words

Lucio is the one to spot something inhuman in Angelo, a lack of judgement in the Duke and, to judge by the Duke's unexpected proposal to Isabella, the Duke's attraction to women. Some scholars wonder if he has nearly guessed the Duke's disguise when he says, 'It was a mad fantastical trick of him to steal from the state and usurp the beggary he was never born to' *(Act 3, Scene 2)*, though the comedy of his subsequent misunderstandings demand that Lucio remains in the dark.

Key quotations

Behold, behold, where Madam Mitigation comes. I have purchased as many diseases under her roof as come to–
(Lucio, Act 1, Scene 2)

Our doubts are traitors
And makes us lose the good we oft might win
(Lucio, Act 1, Scene 4)

Sir, my name is Lucio, well known to the duke.
(Lucio, Act 3, Scene 2)

Activity 5

The audience is aware that the Duke and the 'friar' are the same person whereas Lucio is not. This is an example of dramatic irony in the play. Look closely at the encounters between the Duke and Lucio in Act 3, Scene 2, Act 4, Scene 3 and Act 5, Scene 1. Then describe the effects achieved by the audience being aware of a situation of which Lucio is ignorant.

Escalus

Escalus is a wise and stable counsellor who serves both the Duke and Angelo well, while he is always aware that he must, ultimately, do as commanded. He is sometimes described in character lists as an 'ancient lord'; in Act 1, Scene 1 the Duke calls him 'Old Escalus' and in Act 5, Scene 1, he greets him as 'Our old and faithful friend'. Escalus may be one of a number of lords who fulfil roles in managing the 'city's institutions' of Vienna *(Act 1, Scene 1)*.

His name means 'scales', reminiscent of the scales of justice. He personifies the scales balanced even-handedly between justice and mercy. Like the Duke, he initially expresses a high opinion of Angelo, who he describes as worthy of 'such ample grace and honour' *(Act 1, Scene 1)*. However by Act 2, he begins to express doubts about Angelo's severe judgements and, returning to one of the play's themes, asks if Angelo, who has condemned Claudio for fornication, has not himself 'Err'd in this point' *(Act 2, Scene 1)*. When Angelo becomes impatient with Elbow, Pompey and Froth's court case, it is Escalus who must draw out the particulars and make the final judgements. The theme of justice is also exemplified by Escalus in Act 3, Scene 2, when he is responsible for ordering Mistress Overdone to prison then subsequently discusses the 'severe' judgement on Claudio *(Act 3, Scene 2)*.

In the final act of the play, Escalus is shocked by the revelations of Angelo's misdeeds and the Duke's disguise. He represents a steadfast figure who, though lacking insight into other characters' capacity for disguise and deception, adheres to the expectations of government.

> **Key quotations**
>
> Mercy is not itself that oft looks so,
> Pardon is still the nurse of second woe.
> But yet, poor Claudio; there is no remedy.
> *(Escalus, Act 2, Scene 1)*
>
> My lord, I am more amaz'd at his dishonour,
> Than at the strangeness of it.
> *(Escalus, Act 5, Scene 1)*

> **Activity 6**
>
> In many ways, Lucio and Escalus are opposing figures. One is disrespectful of order, the other respectful; one is punished at the end for insulting the Duke, the other (whose attempt to send the Duke to prison was a mistake due to the Duke's disguise) is pardoned. Use a spider diagram to make notes on both characters and then answer the following question: How do Lucio and Escalus demonstrate the problems and concerns of Vienna?

Pompey

Pompey, an employee of Mistress Overdone, works as a bartender and pimp. He is one of Shakespeare's 'clown' figures, that is, broad comic characters. His name may be ironic as Pompey the Great was an admired political and military leader in the time of Julius Caesar, whereas Escalus declares that Pompey's **'bum is the greatest thing'** about him *(Act 2, Scene 1)*.

Like many clowns, he is a truth-teller, who exposes the vices and corruption of Vienna. His wit is displayed, particularly in Act 2, Scene 1 when, despite annoying Escalus, he escapes with no punishment beyond a warning and in Act 4, Scene 2 when he escapes punishment by becoming the assistant to the executioner. He is literally able to talk himself out of trouble.

> **Key quotations**
>
> I thank your worship for your good counsel; [*Aside*] but I shall follow it as the flesh and fortune shall better determine.
> *(Pompey, Act 2, Scene 1)*
>
> Sir, I will serve him, for I do find your hangman is a more penitent trade than your bawd: he doth oftener ask forgiveness.
> *(Pompey, Act 4, Scene 2)*

Minor characters

Juliet

Juliet is important to the plot of the play but although she appears in three scenes, she only speaks in one. She is Claudio's pregnant lover or, as Claudio puts it, **'fast my wife'** *(Act 1, Scene 2)*. She slept with him because they had a **'true contract'**, which only needed the final arrangements to be made to give the situation **'outward order'** *(Act 1, Scene 2)*. Despite her relative innocence (she loves Claudio and they intend to marry) and her vulnerable condition (she is **'near her hour'** of giving birth *(Act 2, Scene 2)*), she is treated roughly by other characters. She is paraded in the streets with Claudio in Act 1, Scene 2 and Angelo only decrees **'needful'** provisions for her in Act 2, Scene 2. In her prison interview with the Duke, he tells her that her **'sin'** is **'of heavier kind than his'** and reminds her that Claudio **'must die tomorrow'** *(Act 2, Scene 3)*. She asserts that their actions were **'mutually'** committed and repents her **'sin'** *(Act 2, Scene 3)*. She embodies the contrast of the new life within her, which also spares her own life, and the impending death of her love Claudio. Though silent at the end of the play, Claudio is told to **'restore'** her *(Act 5, Scene 1)*.

> **Key quotations**
>
> I do, and bear the shame most patiently.
> *(Juliet, Act 2, Scene 3)*
>
>   Oh, injurious love
> That respites me a life whose very comfort
> Is still a dying horror!
> *(Juliet, Act 2, Scene 3)*

Mariana

For such a small role (she speaks only 2% of the play's lines and does not appear until the play's fourth act), Mariana has inspired the imagination of many readers. Most famously, the poet Alfred Lord Tennyson was inspired by her to write the poem 'Mariana in the Moated Grange' and the artist John Everett Millais painted a version of her surrounded by symbols of her lonely existence. Two key aspects of Mariana seem to appeal to Victorian writers and artists: her loyalty for Angelo and her seclusion in a moated grange. Unlike the urban locations of the other characters, Mariana is outside the city limits in a country home, further isolated

Sir John Everett Millais's painting *Mariana* (1851) emphasizes the character's isolation and weary endurance

by a protective moat. She is first seen listening to a sad love song. These melancholy images of passive feminine suffering may have appealed to Victorian artists, but the other aspect of her character – her ready deception of Angelo in the 'bed-switch' plot – was more shocking.

In Act 5, Scene 1, she pleads eloquently for Angelo and, joined by Isabella, persuades the Duke to spare Angelo's life because **'I crave no other, nor no better man'** *(Act 5, Scene 1).*

Key quotations

Let me excuse me, and believe me so,
My mirth it much displeas'd, but pleas'd my woe.
(Mariana, Act 4, Scene 1)

I have sat here all day.
(Mariana, Act 4, Scene 1)

I hope you will not mock me with a husband?
(Mariana, Act 5, Scene 1)

Activity 7

Read the following stanza of Tennyson's 'Mariana in the Moated Grange' (1830) below and then compare it with the depiction of Mariana in *Measure for Measure*, with particular reference to Act 4, Scene 1.

'Mariana in the Moated Grange'
(Shakespeare, *Measure for Measure*)
by Alfred, Lord Tennyson

With blackest moss the flower-plots
Were thickly crusted, one and all:
The rusted nails fell from the knots
That held the pear to the gable-wall.
The broken sheds look'd sad and strange:
Unlifted was the clinking latch;
Weeded and worn the ancient thatch
Upon the lonely moated grange.
She only said, 'My life is dreary,
He cometh not,' she said;
She said, 'I am aweary, aweary,
I would that I were dead!'

Mistress Overdone

Mistress Overdone runs a taphouse and is a notorious 'bawd', who employs Pompey and entraps naive visitors like Froth. The other characters refer overtly to her illicit activities, with Lucio addressing her as 'Madam Mitigation' *(Act 1, Scene 2)* because she is known for supplying sexual satisfaction. Pompey remarks on her 'service' for which she has almost 'worn' her 'eyes out' *(Act 1, Scene 2)*, a reference to Cupid, the blind god of love. The Provost declares that she has been a 'bawd of eleven years' continuance' *(Act 3, Scene 2)* and there are many references to the diseases that might be caught in her establishment. In Act 1, Scene 2, she bemoans the pulling down of the 'houses of resort in the suburbs' like hers *(Act 1, Scene 2)*. Pompey agrees to help her move to a new location.

In Act 3, Scene 2, she is shown in prison apparently on the evidence of Lucio. She then reveals Lucio's relationship with Kate Keepdown, which resulted in a child. In Act 5, this information is used against Lucio when he is sentenced to be married to Kate.

Key quotations

Thus, what with the war, what with the sweat, what with the gallows, and what with poverty, I am custom-shrunk.
(Mistress Overdone, Act 1, Scene 2)

Why, here's a change indeed in the commonwealth. What shall become of me?
(Mistress Overdone, Act 1, Scene 2)

 Activity 8

Use a table like the one below to compare Juliet, Mariana and Mistress Overdone, and their importance in the play.

Character	Key scenes	Key quotations	Importance to plot
Juliet			
Mariana			
Mistress Overdone			

Provost

The Provost, the keeper of the jail, is an example of a public servant who balances justice with mercy. He is of a lower status than Escalus, but embodies some of the same humanity in his approach to justice. He appears briefly in Act 2, Scene 1, receiving the order to arrange Claudio's execution the next day. In Act 2, Scene 2, he has a brief soliloquy expressing his hope that Angelo will relent. He then has the dual functions of seeking care for Juliet and announcing that Isabella, 'a very virtuous maid', has arrived to speak to Angelo *(Act 2, Scene 2)*. Lucio and he observe the first interview between Angelo and Isabella, both willing Isabella to succeed: 'Pray heaven she win him!' *(Act 2, Scene 2)*. In Acts 3 and 4, he is seen dealing with the diverse characters in the prison, including making the unlikely apprenticeship arrangement between Pompey and Abhorson. In Act 5, his role is primarily one of stage management as he escorts various characters on and off stage.

> **Key quotation**
>
> He hath but as offended in a dream.
>
> All sects, all ages smack of this vice, and he
>
> To die for't?
> *(Provost, Act 2, Scene 2)*

Activity 9

Make a bullet point list with key points and quotations about the Provost in relation to the theme of justice.

Elbow

Elbow is a simple constable who, in Act 2, Scene 1, brings a case against Pompey and Froth. Angelo rapidly loses patience with the constable, whose manner of speaking confuses the case. Constables at this time were usually labourers appointed to this role. They received little money or respect for the role; they often only had their expenses covered, but Elbow says he does it for 'some piece of money' *(Act 2, Scene 1)*, so may receive a little more than that.

Shakespeare had fun with other comic constables, including Dull in *Love's Labour's Lost* and Dogberry in *Much Ado About Nothing* who, though well-intentioned, show themselves to be easily outwitted by others. Their names suggest a comic simplicity and there are several interpretations of the name Elbow. It could suggest that he uses his elbow frequently either to raise a drink or for heavy manual labour, or he might get to places by zig-zagging or not going in a straight line (that is, crooked like an elbow). This last suggests the indirect and complicated way Elbow presents his complaint. He is particularly agitated as he believes his wife's reputation has been sullied either by people thinking he had pre-marital sex with her or by the attentions of Froth.

Elbow demonstrates how inefficient the law is in Vienna and Escalus gently suggests that there might be others in Elbow's parish who might be 'sufficient' to serve in his place *(Act 2, Scene 1)*. However, Elbow redeems himself in Act 3, Scene 2 by successfully bringing Pompey to the prison for being a bawd ('buy and sell men and women like beasts' *(Act 3, Scene 2)*) and for being possessed of a pick-lock, indicating that Pompey is also a thief.

> **Key quotation**
>
> If it please your honour, I am the poor duke's constable, and my name is Elbow. I do lean upon justice, sir, and do bring in here, before your good honour, two notorious benefactors.
> *(Elbow, Act 2, Scene 1)*

Activity 10

Elbow's wife, like Kate Keepdown, is a female character who is mentioned in the play but does not appear. Write a paragraph in response to the following question: What is the importance of unseen characters, like Elbow's wife and Kate Keepdown, to the plot of *Measure for Measure*?

Tips for assessment

In order to make clear you are writing about characters who have been created by a playwright, rather than about real people, consider using phrases like, 'Shakespeare presents Elbow as...' or 'Shakespeare contrasts Elbow with...'.

Abhorson

Abhorson, the executioner, is another of the play's comic characters. In Act 4, Scene 2, he is brought on to interview Pompey for the job of assistant executioner. He initially rejects Pompey because he is a 'bawd' who will disgrace the role of executioner, which is a specialist occupation, or, as Abhorson repeatedly puts it, 'a mystery' *(Act 4, Scene 2)*. After a comic dialogue in which Pompey puns on various mysteries, Abhorson accepts Pompey as his assistant: 'Come on, bawd. I will instruct thee in my trade' *(Act 4, Scene 2)*. In the following scene, Abhorson sends for Barnardine to be executed. Barnardine greets him casually but refuses to go to the executioner's block.

Despite his violent profession, Abhorson is presented as a stolid man who takes pride in his work and follows the instructions of his superiors. He has a simple belief in the worth and dignity of his occupation.

Activity 11

Use the spider diagram to revise the main 'prison characters' and their importance to the play.

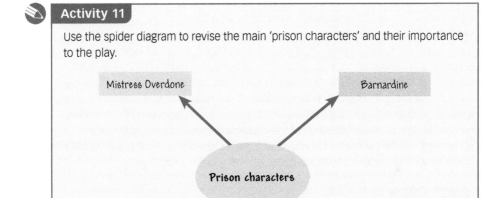

Froth

Froth is a young man whose recently deceased father has left him comfortably off financially: **'a man of four score pound a year'** *(Act 2, Scene 1)*. He admits he is attracted to taphouses: **'it is an open room, and good for winter'** *(Act 2, Scene 1)*. Sensing that Froth is likely to get in trouble if he continues to associate with Pompey and Mistress Overdone, he is ordered by Escalus to stay away. Froth is often portrayed as a frivolous character (the word 'froth' means unsubstantial). The 2004 Complicite production portrayed Froth as having curly hair, reminiscent of the froth on a beer. He admits to being drawn into taphouses, a wordplay on beer which is drawn from a tap, or people who are enticed or tricked.

Key quotation

For mine own part, I never come into any room in a taphouse, but I am drawn in.
(Froth, Act 2, Scene 1)

Barnardine

As a character, Barnardine's purpose seems to be to test the limits of justice and mercy in Vienna, as well as the patience of those who work in the prison.

He is scheduled to be executed on the same day as Claudio and he is used as a direct contrast to Claudio. For example, Claudio deserves **'pity'** and Barnardine **'not a jot'** *(Act 4, Scene 2)*. Barnardine is a murderer who has been a prisoner for nine years and it is a sign of the Duke's previous laxness that in all that time he hadn't **'delivered him to his liberty or executed him'** *(Act 4, Scene 2)*. Unlike Claudio, Barnardine is indifferent to death and prison, but the plot to switch his head with Claudio's to send to Angelo is thwarted by his assertion that he has been drinking and therefore is in no fit state to be executed. A 'barnard' was a Jacobean word for a decoy, so Shakespeare may have been alluding to the substitution of Barnardine for Claudio. The Christian attitudes of the characters is demonstrated by their agreement that he cannot be beheaded when he is not in a state of grace. At the end of the play, he is pardoned by the Duke, which he accepts with silence.

> **Key quotation**
>
> **I have been drinking hard all night, and I will have more time to prepare me, or they shall beat out my brains with billets. I will not consent to die this day, that's certain.**
> *(Barnardine, Act 4, Scene 3)*

Activity 12

Barnardine is presented as an unthinking man: **'careless, reckless, and fearless of what's past, present, or to come: insensible of mortality and desperately mortal'** *(Act 4, Scene 2)*. Make a bullet point list contrasting his attitudes to life, the law and death with those of Claudio, Isabella and Angelo.

Francisca

Francisca is a nun in the Convent of Saint Clare. She is not allowed to answer the door of the convent as her vows forbid informal contact with men. Francisca explains the severe life that Isabella has chosen and that Isabella wishes was **'more strict'** *(Act 1, Scene 4)*. As a character, Francisca can be contrasted with Mistress Overdone, whose occupation depends on contact with many men.

Friar Thomas

In Act 1, Scene 3, the Duke confides in Friar Thomas his plot to observe how Angelo rules Vienna by assuming the habit of a **'true friar'** *(Act 1, Scene 3)*. Friar Thomas is sympathetic to this plan, saying that the justice would be **'more dreadful'** from the Duke than Angelo *(Act 1, Scene 3)*. His figure is parallel to that of Francisca the nun who instructs Isabella in Act 1, Scene 4.

Friar Peter

Friar Peter appears in Acts 4 and 5 to assist the plot's resolution by delivering letters; arranging where Isabella and others will stand when the Duke arrives; contradicting Lucio's account of Friar Lodowick (the Duke's assumed name as a friar); and presumably carrying out the multiple marriages at the play's conclusion.

Justice

Justice is an assistant to Escalus who, in Act 2, Scene 1 states that 'Lord Angelo is severe' *(Act 2, Scene 1).*

Two Gentlemen

The two unnamed gentlemen appear in Act 1, Scene 2 to trade insults and jokes with Lucio, providing a sense of the concerns and habits of the citizens of Vienna.

Activity 13

'Shakespeare populates *Measure for Measure* with a colourful collection of minor characters to demonstrate both the vices and virtues of Vienna.' Choose a selection of the minor characters and write a paragraph explaining how they portray both the best and worst of Vienna.

Writing about characterization and roles

When writing about characters and characterization, remember to do the following:

- Discuss the characters as constructions of the playwright, not as real people.
- Discuss the different ways a character can be interpreted.
- Consider which themes a character may be used to explore, such as justice, religion or desire.
- Think about the character's role and function in the play.
- Analyse how the character is developed throughout the play.
- Consider not only what characters say and do but how other characters perceive them.
- Note if the characters use language in a specific way, such as verse or prose, or particular imagery or wordplay.
- Reflect on how the context of the play may influence how the characters are understood.

The plays are full of double-meanings, slips of the tongue and puns. In a period that valued rhetoric as an expression of scholarship, the plays constantly reflect upon the power of speech itself and its potential for deception as well as truth: language seems less a transparent medium for 'truth' and more a complex of variations and uncertainties of meaning.

(Simon Barker, 'Introduction', *Shakespeare's Problem Plays: Contemporary Critical Essays*)

Language is at the heart of Shakespeare's plays. He rarely relied on large visual effects; instead the appeal was mainly aural. In his age, audiences would refer to going to 'hear' rather than 'see' a play and they were attuned to listening to speeches and dialogue. Shakespeare was known for his particular skill at bringing thoughts and words together. In *Measure for Measure*, language is used as a tool to win an argument, subdue an adversary or to baffle a judge.

Prose and verse

Measure for Measure is written largely in blank verse, in unrhymed lines of **iambic pentameter**, the form preferred by most Elizabethan playwrights. Iambic pentameter consists of lines of ten syllables, alternating unstressed and stressed syllables. Roughly two-thirds of the play is written in verse. The play begins in verse, with the Duke's formal announcement to Escalus of his plans, but switches to prose in Act 1, Scene 2 to capture the casual street conversations of Lucio and his companions. However, when Claudio arrives to explain his arrest, Shakespeare switches back to verse:

> **Key quotation**
>
> Like rats that ravin down their proper bane
> (Claudio, Act 1, Scene 2)

Regular iambic pentameter, like the line above, has five feet (or iambs) of verse, consisting of an unstressed syllable followed by a stressed one (underlined). However not all of the verse is regular; some lines contain fewer or more than ten syllables, some end with a stressed syllable and some not.

In some scenes, lines of verse are split between characters:

> **Key quotation**
>
> Angelo: I will not do't.
>
> Isabella: But can you if you would?
> (Act 2, Scene 2)

Note that 'do it' has been **elided** in order to make it one syllable ('do't'), so as to fit the metre and that Isabella picks up the line of verse directly from Angelo, suggesting that there would be no pause when she continues the line.

If Isabella follows the iambic pentameter pattern, it suggests that she would stress the words 'can' and ' if' rather than 'you', meaning that she is seeking to know how much power or agency Angelo has (or could choose to have) in this situation.

In some lines, Shakespeare has used a **caesura** to suggest a pause in the verse. At the end of Act 4, Scene 4, Angelo's soliloquy contains several caesuras. There is a full stop in the second line before the phrase 'A deflower'd maid', perhaps suggesting his realization of the enormity of what he has done. There are full stops before 'He should have liv'd' and 'Would yet he had liv'd' as if he regrets his responsibility for what he believes was Claudio's execution. As well as the pauses, more irregular line lengths, with some lines having 11 beats and others 9, suggest the broken, fragmented nature of his thoughts as he alternates between justifications for his actions and his guilt.

Another use of pause occurs in Act 5, Scene 1, when Isabella's iambic pentameter lines are interrupted by a line with only four syllables: 'For Angelo'. Some actors playing Isabella employ a long pause, as long as six beats, before beginning the next line in order to show how difficult it is for her to plead for mercy for Angelo after everything he has done.

The Duke speaks some of the most extended formal verse in the play, though he also uses prose, for example, in his interactions with Lucio. Other characters of status, such as Angelo and Isabella, also speak primarily in verse. The formality of their speech is highlighted by the occasional use of **rhyming couplets** at the end of scenes. The final words of the final two lines are emphasized by the use of rhyme and may bring about a sense of conclusion or resolution.

> **caesura** a pause or break near the middle of a line of verse
>
> **elided** merged
>
> **iambic pentameter** lines of verse consisting of five feet (iambs), each consisting of one unstressed and one stressed syllable
>
> **rhyming couplet** two consecutive lines of verse, which rhyme

 Activity 1

Skim read Act 1 and note when the dialogue is in verse and when in prose. Try to identify if any characters or situations are more associated with verse than others.

Activity 2

Study the rhyming couplets below and explain what they mean and how they support the play's plot and themes.

Is more to bread than stone. Hence shall we see,
If power change purpose, what our seemers be.
(Duke, Act 1, Scene 3)

Subdues me quite. Ever till now
When men were fond, I smil'd, and wondered how.
(Angelo, Act 2, Scene 2)

I'll tell him yet of Angelo's request,
And fit his mind to death for his soul's rest.
(Isabella, Act 2, Scene 4)

Pay with falsehood false exacting
And perform an old contracting.
(Duke, Act 3, Scene 2)

Let me excuse me, and believe me so,
My mirth it much displeas'd, but pleas'd my woe.
(Mariana, Act 4, Scene 1)

Dialogue and soliloquies

The play contains dialogue, when two or more characters are conversing; speeches, when one character speaks an extended number of lines addressed to one or more other characters, such as a public declaration; and soliloquies, when characters are alone on stage sharing their thoughts with the audience.

When analysing a scene, it is worth noting if one character dominates the scene by having most of the lines, if there is a particular rhythm to the lines or if words or imagery are repeated or shared between characters. Usually dialogue is addressed to other characters on stage, but it may be punctuated with **asides**, when a character makes a short remark directly to the audience.

Soliloquies are frequently spoken directly to the audience, allowing the character to open a window into their innermost thoughts and feelings. Some actors consciously include the audience in their soliloquies, looking to them for sympathy or advice, while others choose to enact the soliloquies in a more introspective way, as if speaking to themselves.

At the end of Act 3, Scene 2, the Duke reflects on how Angelo will be judged as harshly as he has judged others

Activity 3

a) Study Act 2, Scene 2 and note the following:

- In what sections of the scene does Isabella have the most lines? When does Angelo have the most lines? When are the lines evenly shared between the two?

- What is the effect of the asides from Lucio and the Provost?

b) In Act 2, Scene 4, what is the effect of the brevity of some of Isabella's responses, like **'So'** or **'True'**? How does this affect the rhythm of the scene?

Rhetoric

Rhetoric, the art of debate and persuasion, was taught in schools during the Elizabethan age, and Shakespeare uses rhetorical techniques in the central debates in the play. Aristotle identified three elements in rhetoric:

- **Ethos:** the speaker shows their reliability, morality or authority
- **Pathos:** the speaker makes an appeal to emotion
- **Logos:** the speaker uses logic, such as providing examples or evidence.

An example of ethos occurs in Act 2, Scene 2, where Isabella establishes her own virtue declaring that Claudio's sin is **'a vice that most I do abhor'**. Later in the scene, she uses pathos when appealing to Angelo's emotions, saying that nothing becomes a judge so much **'As mercy does'**. She later employs logos when she argues that Claudio is **'not prepar'd for death'** and asks **'Who is it that hath died for this offence?'** *(Act 2, Scene 2)*.

Two common rhetorical devices used in *Measure for Measure* are **anaphora** and **rhetorical questions**. In Act 5, Scene 1, Isabella uses both techniques:

Key quotation

That Angelo's forsworn, is it not strange?
That Angelo's a murderer, is't not strange?
That Angelo is an adulterous thief,
An hypocrite, a virgin-violator,
Is it not strange, and strange?
(Isabella, Act 5, Scene 1)

anaphora the repetition of key phrases at the beginning of a line or sentence to create a dramatic effect

aside brief lines spoken by actors and addressed to the audience rather than the other characters on stage

rhetorical question a question asked to achieve an effect rather than to receive a reply

Activity 4

Analysing Isabella's lines on page 65, consider what is the effect of the anaphoric phrase 'That Angelo...'? What effect would the questions have on Angelo and others listening? What is the importance of her repetition of the word 'strange'?

Another aspect of rhetoric is the organization of ideas. In Act 5, Scene 1, Mariana reveals herself in three stages, using the anaphoric repetition of 'This is' while itemizing the contract between Angelo and her by referencing her 'face', 'hand' and 'body'.

Antithesis is also used to demonstrate two sides of an argument or the stark choices facing the characters. When Claudio states 'Death is a fearful thing', Isabella points out its antithesis, that a 'shamed life [is] a hateful' one *(Act 3, Scene 1)*. She again contrasts living and dying when she declares, 'Then Isabel live chaste, and brother die' *(Act 2, Scene 4)* and Angelo points out antithetically, 'my false o'erweighs your true' *(Act 2, Scene 4)*.

alliteration the repetition of the initial sound or letter of words

antithesis placing a statement and an opposing statement in the same sentence

extended metaphor when a metaphoric comparison continues for a few lines or sentences

metaphor a figure of speech applied to something to suggest a resemblance, without using the words 'like' or 'as'

simile a figure of speech when two things are compared, using the words 'like' or 'as'

Alliteration

Throughout the play, Shakespeare uses **alliteration** to create memorable phrases. When analysing alliteration, think about the effect of the repeated sounds and if they make the phrase sound more frightening, comic or dramatic.

For example, a 'dribbling dart of love' *(Act 1, Scene 3)* sounds comic or derisive when the Duke is explaining to the Friar that he is not in disguise due to a secret love assignation (the darts refer to arrows from Cupid, the god of love). In contrast, the alliterative 'marble monument' *(Act 5, Scene 1)* sounds reassuringly solid and strong.

Activity 5

Analyse the examples of alliteration below and explain the effect they have.

Example of alliteration	Effect
Mortality and mercy (Duke, Act 1, Scene 1)	
foppery of freedom (Lucio, Act 1, Scene 2)	
prince and people (Duke, Act 1, Scene 3)	
heading and hanging (Escalus, Act 2, Scene 1)	
flesh and fortune (Pompey, Act 2, Scene 1)	
fiery floods (Claudio, Act 3, Scene 1)	
promised proportions (Angelo, Act 5, Scene 1)	
foolish friar (Duke, Act 5, Scene 1)	

Imagery

Metaphors

Throughout the play the dialogue is enriched with imagery. For example, in Act 1, Scene 2, a series of images associated with tailoring are used to describe Lucio's character. After Lucio calls the First Gentleman 'a villain', the First Gentleman retorts that there is 'but a pair of shears' between them, meaning that they are the same, as they are cut from the same cloth. Lucio uses the **metaphor** of 'velvet', a fine, luxurious fabric, to describe himself, whereas the gentleman is only 'list' or the rough edges of the cloth. The metaphor is extended by the First Gentleman, who claims he would rather be a plain English cloth like 'kersey' than worn ('piled') 'French velvet'. Later in the same scene, Claudio uses the metaphor of a horse to describe the public, which Angelo (as the governor) must ride, letting it feel his 'spur'. This metaphor shows Claudio's insight into Angelo being 'newly in the seat', that is, unused to power and therefore unreasonably severe *(Act 1, Scene 2)*.

Activity 6

Act 2, Scene 1 begins with the metaphor of a **'scarecrow'** for the **'law'**. Explain what we learn about Angelo's attitude towards the law from this **extended metaphor**.

Similes

Similes are also comparisons but they use the words 'like' or 'as' to draw attention to the similarities. In *Measure for Measure*, similes are often used to make criticisms such as comparing the unused penalties in Vienna to 'unscour'd armour' (a soldier's protective armour) *(Act 1, Scene 2)*, which has hung unused on a wall, or Isabella's complaint about the frailty and vanity of women when she replies to Angelo that they are 'as the glasses [mirrors] where they view themselves, / Which are as easy broke as they make forms' *(Act 2, Scene 4)*.

Personification

The use of **personification** is a way of making concepts active and concrete. Mistress Overdone, who is dubbed 'Madam Mitigation' *(Act 1, Scene 2)*, becomes a walking embodiment of sexual satisfaction. Nature is compared to a 'thrifty goddess' *(Act 1, Scene 1)* and 'Liberty plucks Justice by the nose' *(Act 1, Scene 3)*, personifying the war between desire and the law in Vienna. Escalus claims that Angelo has forced him to tell him 'he is indeed Justice' *(Act 3, Scene 2)*, that is, not to be questioned because as he is justice personified, so his word is law.

Activity 7

a) Copy and annotate the following speech by the Duke to locate examples of the following:

- alliteration
- personification
- simile
- metaphor.

> We have strict statutes and most biting laws,
> The needful bits and curbs to headstrong weeds,
> Which for this fourteen years we have let slip,
> Even like an o'er-grown lion in a cave
> That goes not out to prey. Now, as fond fathers
> Having bound up the threatening twigs of birch
> Only to stick it in their children's sight
> For terror, not to use – in time the rod
> More mock'd than fear'd – so our decrees,
> Dead to infliction, to themselves are dead,
> And Liberty plucks Justice by the nose,
> The baby beats the nurse, and quite athwart
> Goes all decorum.
> *(Duke, Act 1, Scene 3)*

b) Write a paragraph explaining how the language in the Duke's speech portrays Vienna's laws and the public's reactions to them.

irony words that express the opposite of what is meant; the difference between what may be expected and what actually occurs

personification when human qualities are attributed to something non-human such as an object or idea

Nature imagery

Nature imagery occurs in several key scenes, such as Claudio's horse imagery in Act 1, Scene 2, Lucio's depiction of Angelo's blood as 'very snow-broth' (Act 1, Scene 4) or Isabella's description of Angelo's garden in Act 4, Scene 1: 'He hath a garden circummur'd with brick'.

Act 2, Scene 2 is a particularly rich scene for exploring Shakespeare's use of nature imagery, as Isabella uses it to support her argument for her brother's life and Angelo employs it to describe his own corruption.

> ### Activity 8
>
> Read the quotations below and then use them in a paragraph explaining what effects are achieved through the use of nature imagery in Act 2, Scene 2.
>
> - **We kill the fowl of season**
>   (Isabella)
>
> - **Thou rather with thy sharp and sulphurous bolt / Splits the unwedgable and gnarled oak / Than the soft myrtle**
>   (Isabella)
>
> - **… lying by the violet in the sun, / Do as the carrion does, not as the flower, / Corrupt with virtuous season**
>   (Angelo)

Irony and paradox

Many critics consider *Measure for Measure* a deeply ironic play. One definition of **irony** is when the state of events is deliberately contrary to expectations, causing surprise, confusion or amusement. Vienna is a topsy-turvy world where a powerful Duke disguises himself as a poor friar, then appoints an apparently upright deputy (the ironically named Angelo), who turns out to be a lecher, and the justice system is so chaotic that murderers like Barnardine can defy their executioners.

Dramatic irony is also frequently employed. The audience is aware that Lucio is insulting the Duke to his face and Shakespeare emphasizes this irony by having the Duke, dressed as a friar, say, 'if ever the duke return, as our prayers are he may, let me desire you to make your answer before him' (Act 3, Scene 2). This heightens the audience's anticipation of Lucio's ultimate comeuppance.

A more ominous use of dramatic irony occurs when the audience knows that Claudio has not been executed, but the Duke allows other characters, such as Isabella and Angelo, to believe he has. When Angelo says 'He should have liv'd' (Act 4, Scene 4), the audience knows that Claudio is alive but still judges Angelo for his intentions, where tragedy was only averted by the Duke's plan.

At points, Shakespeare draws attention to the theatricality and performance aspects of the play. Early in the play, the Duke makes a **meta-theatrical** declaration:

> **Key quotation**
>
> I love the people,
> But do not like to stage me to their eyes:
> Though it do well I do not relish well
> Their loud applause
> *(Duke, Act 1, Scene 1)*

This is ironic as these words are spoken by an actor on a stage who, at the end of the play, will seek the audience's applause. The irony is compounded by the Duke's very public resolution of the play, odd for someone who claims he doesn't want to submit himself to 'their eyes'. In Act 5, Scene 1, he also urges Lucio to 'Be perfect', an Elizabethan term for an actor knowing their lines and possibly a reprimand to the comic actor playing the role, as Elizabethan comics were known to **ad-lib** lines.

Another type of irony is to state the opposite of what is expected, such as Escalus's description of the simple and confused Elbow as a 'wise officer' *(Act 2, Scene 1)* or Claudio's account of the murderer Barnardine 'in sleep as guiltless labour' *(Act 4, Scene 2)*.

The play is rich in paradox, where seemingly contradictory or impossible statements are made. For example, Claudio says that he will 'sue to live, I find I seek to die, / And seeking death, find life' *(Act 3, Scene 1)*. Isabella uses an **oxymoron** to describe Angelo: 'There is a devilish mercy in the judge' *(Act 3, Scene 1)*.

Activity 9

Look at the quotations below and then write a line describing the use of irony in each one.

Example	Explanation of irony
Escalus: ... Is it a lawful trade? Pompey: If the law would allow it, sir. *(Act 2, Scene 1)*	
Pompey the Great *(Escalus, Act 2, Scene 1)*	
Oh, you hope the duke will return no more? *(Duke, Act 3, Scene 2)*	
That is your part... *(Isabella, Act 4, Scene 6)*	

Wordplay

Characters in the play often use words creatively, such as using puns and sexual innuendo for comic effect, but also, at times, to uncover the darker concerns of the play. Act 1, Scene 2 is particularly rich in wordplay. When Mistress Overdone enters, Lucio refers to the diseases that may be purchased 'under her roof' (Act 1, Scene 2) and goes on to reference syphilis in many coded ways:

- 'A French crown' refers both to crowns, the money of the period, but also to the 'French disease', as the English referred to syphilis.
- 'Thy bones are hollow' is another reference to the symptoms of syphilis, which Lucio uses in reply to the First Gentleman's claim to be sound, as in 'sound as a bell', which is also hollow.
- Throughout, the characters use the language of finance to discuss the purchasing of sexual favours: 'purchased', 'figuring', 'full of error'.

Pompey uses wordplay in Act 2, Scene 1, playing with the double meaning of the word 'longing' when he describes Mistress Elbow as 'longing' for prunes, but also suggesting sexual desires. Pompey claims that nothing was 'done' (an ambiguous word with a sexual undertone) to Elbow's wife 'once', which may mean that it did not happen at all – or occurred many times.

Wordplay is used to discuss serious subjects like death. The **euphemism** of sleep for death is used by Pompey when he advises Barnardine to 'awake till you are executed, and sleep afterwards' (Act 4, Scene 3). The Duke tells Isabella that Angelo hath 'releas'd' Claudio (Act 4, Scene 3), which could be interpreted either as he has freed him or he has killed him thereby releasing him from his earthly troubles.

---

ad-lib unscripted words, said without preparation

euphemism an indirect or more positive way of expressing something unpleasant or harsh

meta-theatrical theatre that draws attention to its own artifice, e.g. by pointing out that it is a play rather than reality

oxymoron a figure of speech containing an essential contradiction, such as 'hot ice' or 'joyous sorrow'

 Activity 10

Analyse the effects of the wordplay below:

Pompey: Yonder man is carried to prison.
Mistress Overdone: Well, what has he done?
Pompey: A woman.
(Act 1, Scene 2)

Mistress Overdone: ... Is there a maid with child by him?
Pompey: No, but there's a woman with maid by him.
(Act 1, Scene 2)

Malapropisms

One of the sources of humour in the play, particularly Act 2, Scene 1, is the use of **malapropisms**. The constable Elbow arrives full of righteous indignation but is unable to make his complaint clear due to his use of similar sounding but incorrect words, a trait he shares with another of Shakespeare's constables, Dogberry in *Much Ado About Nothing*.

Activity 11

Look at what Elbow says in Act 2, Scene 1 and then put the correct word and meaning in the adjoining box.

What Elbow says	What he means
two notorious benefactors	malefactors: someone who commits a crime
My wife, sir, whom I detest	
if she had been a woman cardinally	
that she was ever respected with man, woman or child	

malapropism using an incorrect word for another, often creating a comic effect

Names

Shakespeare's use of names is particularly colourful in *Measure for Measure*. Mistress Overdone's name suggests a life of over-indulgence, including having, and apparently outliving, nine husbands. It could also rudely imply that she herself has been 'done' over and over again. The unseen mother of Lucio's baby, the alliteratively named Kate Keepdown, may be kept down by her lowly station in life. She shares her first name with the ill-tempered Kate in *The Taming of the Shrew*, possibly suggesting that it is her temperament as well as her profession that makes Lucio unwilling to marry her. At the root of the executioner Abhorson's name is 'abhors', meaning to view with disgust, which many might feel about the executioner's job. The sound of his name also echoes the insult 'whore's son'.

Juliet shares her name with the heroine of *Romeo and Juliet,* another impulsive young lover. Mariana's name derives from Mary, the virgin mother of Christ, and she shows a patient fortitude associated with Mary, though this analysis of her name may sit uneasily with her deflowering by Angelo.

Activity 12

In Act 4, Scene 3, Pompey introduces many of the inhabitants of the prison, such as Master Rash, Master Caper and Master Forthright. After reading the speech, make a note of what you learn about each of the prisoners and whether their name reflects their personality, their job or their crime. For example, someone who is 'rash' acts on impulse, so what has Master Rash impulsively done to end up in prison?

Abhorson is often portrayed in a comic way to match his name

Writing about language

Analysis of language is essential to writing well about the play. When checking over your work, ensure that you have:

- used correct literary terminology, such as 'prose', 'imagery' or 'irony'
- explained the effect of the literary techniques, such as providing insight into the characters, adding humour or enhancing themes
- provided short, well-selected quotations to support your points
- considered what the characters' dialogue or soliloquies reveal about them
- analysed how rhetorical techniques were used in scenes of persuasion
- reflected upon how Shakespeare uses language to create the different worlds of the play.

Shakespeare's play explores many fascinating themes, such as justice, mercy, marriage and death. The themes are revealed through Shakespeare's use of imagery, plot, characterization and setting.

Authority

 ... one of the main, basic – almost obsessional – Shakespearian themes: that of a good and a bad ruler, of the usurper who deprives the legal prince of his throne. This is Shakespeare's view of history, eternal history, its perpetual, unchanging mechanism. It is repeated in the Histories and in the Tragedies – in *Hamlet* and *Macbeth* – even in the comedies, for this theme is present in *Measure for Measure* and in *As You Like It*.

(Jan Kott, *Shakespeare Our Contemporary*)

 Rank and power, like wit and beauty, are but lent, and interest must be paid...

(Germaine Greer, *Shakespeare*)

In *Measure for Measure*, the Duke is the figure of authority who makes the controversial decision temporarily to abdicate his responsibilities in favour of the untested Angelo. While Kott highlights figures like Claudius in *Hamlet* or Macbeth in *Macbeth*, who kill a king in order to obtain the throne, the Duke may bear more resemblance to the title character of *King Lear* who, misreading the characters of his children, hands his power to them only to discover that those who grasp it prove unworthy of his trust. In the 17th century, when questions of succession to the throne were always topical, this voluntary relinquishing of power is a striking act. The Duke, who is unmarried and childless, at once seems to be considering his own limitations as a ruler but also to be seeking an heir to his dukedom. However, he is unable to retreat totally and instead goes undercover, in the disguise of a poor friar, in order to judge Angelo's qualities as a ruler and, when necessary, to intervene.

Throughout the play, Shakespeare asks the question, 'What makes a good ruler?' The Duke has laws that he does not enforce, leading to a city teeming with corruption, while Angelo enforces the laws without any mercy, choosing first to punish those who seem to be least deserving of it. Shakespeare may also be examining the corrupting qualities of power. The Duke only sees his kingdom clearly once he removes himself from power and Angelo's cruelty and lechery are released only when he has the power to impose them on others. Some modern productions choose to emphasize the hypocrisy and corruption of politicians, particularly in their portrayals of Angelo.

In Act 1, Scene 2, Claudio refers to the 'demi-god, Authority', which requires him to 'pay down for our offence' and, although not all are similarly punished he declares, "tis just'. In contrast, Isabella speaks more critically of authority. She asserts that the trappings of authority ('the king's crown', 'the judge's robe') are not as significant as mercy (*Act 2, Scene 2*). A source of humour in the play is seeing those in power humbled, as when the Duke must suffer Lucio's insults or Pompey's irreverent replies to Escalus.

Activity 1

In Act 2, Scene 2, Isabella criticizes men who lose their humanity by their behaviour when given 'a little brief authority'. Read the speech and note the specific words and phrases she uses to criticize the behaviour of Angelo and other men who suddenly discover they have power.

Key quotation

Lent him our terror, dress'd him with our love,
And given his deputation all the organs
Of our own power.

(Duke, Act 1, Scene 1)

Justice and mercy

 … just as certainly as *Hamlet* was a play of revenge, so was *Promos and Cassandra* [the source of *Measure for Measure*] a play of forgiveness.

(R.W. Chambers, *Measure for Measure in Shakespeare the Comedies*)

 Measure for Measure is about seeming justice in conflict with the rank reality of sex: about honour in the guise of 'the demi-god Authority'.

(A.P. Rossiter, 'The Problem Plays', *Shakespeare: Modern Essays in Criticism*)

Some critics view the play as being so cynical that it depicts a world in which there is no justice. However there is no question that justice and mercy are among the play's constant preoccupations. The play opens with the Duke relinquishing his rule of the 'city's institutions' and 'the terms / For common justice'. He has 'lent' Angelo his 'terror' to enforce the city's laws (*Act 1, Scene 1*).

In Act 1, Scene 3, the Duke explains to the Friar that the 'strict statutes' and 'biting laws' are 'More mock'd than fear'd', so he hopes that Angelo will be able to restore order. In Act 2, Scene 1, Angelo sets out his determination not to 'make a scarecrow of the law'. This metaphor shows how ineffective laws have been previously in Vienna as they are now so disregarded that 'birds of prey' make the scarecrow 'Their perch' rather than being frightened by it. He uses another metaphor, 'The jewel' *(Act 2, Scene 1)*, to explain that they must act on what they see. This means that Juliet's visible pregnancy makes it right that Claudius and she are arrested, even if there are many others who committed the same crime with no visible evidence.

The loftier discussions of the law and justice are countered by the comic court case brought by Elbow against Pompey and Froth. After Elbow and Pompey's long and complicated explanation of the case, Escalus appears to use his own common sense rather than the letter of law in his judgement. Froth is advised to avoid tapsters in the future; Pompey is warned he will be whipped if he comes before Escalus again; and Elbow is gently questioned if there is someone else from his parish who would be a more suitable constable. Although it is easy to be sympathetic with Escalus's response, it also shows how ineffective the court system is: neither Pompey nor Froth seem inclined to change their ways and, in Act 3, Scene 2, Elbow is still acting as the constable.

The play also focuses on the punishment of those who are convicted. In Shakespeare's time, fornication was often punished by being shamed. In Act 1, Scene 2, Claudio and Juliet are humiliated in the street with Claudio asking, 'why dost thou show me thus to th'world'. Some productions emphasize the humiliation of the lovers.

One production had Juliet wearing a sign around her neck with the word 'Fornicatress' written on it, which is echoed in Angelo's description of her in Act 2, Scene 2. The scenes in prison show the range of characters imprisoned for a variety of offences from debt to murder. The figure of Abhorson and the frequent references to the chopping 'block' reinforce the idea that death will provide the ultimate judgement on the characters.

Mariana begs the Duke to show mercy to Angelo

The other side of justice is mercy. Even those, like Isabella and Escalus, who believe the law against fornication is just, plead for leniency in the case of Claudio, who intends to marry Juliet. Act 5, Scene 1 can be read as an attempt to balance justice with mercy. Isabella pleads for justice for the wrongs that Angelo has done her (so vehemently at one point that she repeats the word 'justice' four times), yet this is then countered by Mariana and her pleas for mercy for Angelo later in the act. The Duke eventually hands out his version of justice and mercy, with Lucio the only character to be punished, possibly becoming the scapegoat for the sins of all the other characters.

Activity 2

Use the spider diagram below to analyse the different examples of justice in the play. Find at least one quotation to support each example.

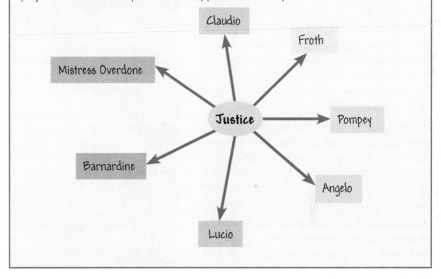

Key quotation

Till you have heard me in my true complaint
And given me justice, justice, justice, justice!
(Isabella, Act 5, Scene 1)

Tips for assessment

When writing about themes, remember to note different instances when a theme is explored in the play. A theme is a big idea, so will not occur just once.

Appearance and reality

Disguise is a recurring feature in Shakespeare's plays, particularly in his comedies. While in disguise, the Duke learns some hard truths about how some of his citizens view him but he also rediscovers his desire to rule Vienna.

In disguise, the Duke meets Isabella and decides to marry her. Disguise is also an essential element of the 'bed-switch', when Mariana impersonates Isabella in order to trick Angelo into consummating their relationship. She is disguised again when she enters wearing a veil in order to serve as a witness against Angelo. Mariana then dramatically unveils herself in order to confront Angelo with the reality of his actions.

Throughout the play, there is a tension between public and private identity. The Angelo that the public sees is very different from the man tormented by sexual desire and his own guilty conscience as revealed in his soliloquies. In contrast to his severe public appearance as an unrelenting 'Justice', in private he is torn between what he should do and what he wants: 'What dost thou or what art thou, Angelo?' (Act 2, Scene 2). He appears to receive the news of Claudio's supposed execution calmly but in private admits 'This deed unshapes me quite' (Act 4, Scene 5). Angelo's hypocrisy in judging others harshly for crimes that he is willing to commit himself is referenced in the play's title. In Act 5, Scene 1, the public setting of the city gates brings into light all the crimes that were occurring in the dark corners of Vienna and the characters are reintegrated into an easily identifiable social construction, the hierarchy is restored and sexual desires are ordered into married pairs.

Angelo's behaviour towards Isabella in Act 2, Scene 4 is often portrayed aggressively, as in the 2006 production at the Theatre Royal in Bath

Activity 3

Write a paragraph in response to the following question: How does Shakespeare use the public setting of the city gates of Vienna to help resolve the theme of reality versus appearance in *Measure for Measure*?

Gender, sex and marriage

 So among the many moral and social issues in *Measure for Measure*, a lover's subjective imagination is again presented and the judgements dependent on the ideal of love's order are again implicit in its action: the duke believes he is 'complete' without love, but at the end asks for love; Angelo and Isabella attempt to establish some order in the affairs of love by 'restraint', the one by caring about the appearance of strict chastity and righteousness, the other by entering a nunnery, and both regimens are tested and found wanting […] Earlier comedies had celebrated the fulfilment of love's order, but this play explores the difficulty with which any such order is attained, and the good intentions of those who fail to achieve it.

(John Russell Brown, 'Love's Ordeal', *Shakespeare and his Comedies*)

The play presents the conflict between chastity and sex, life and death. On one hand, the chaste Isabella is pitted against the sexual incontinence of characters ranging from Mistress Overdone to her own brother Claudio, who describes the lust to which he and Juliet have submitted as 'A thirsty evil' *(Act 1, Scene 2)*. Angelo presents himself as someone who abstains from sex but finds his desires overcome within minutes of meeting Isabella. The unrestrained, disruptive sexuality of the brothel characters is contrasted with the marriage arrangements of the well-born characters, with their complex understandings, pre-contracts and dowries. In Act 5, Scene 1, Mariana is questioned if she is 'married', 'a maid' or 'a widow', to which Lucio offers a fourth possibility – 'a punk', or a whore. It is in the context of these choices, that Isabella chooses to become a nun, thus removing herself from the other roles available to women.

In the underworld, sex is equated with disease, with many puns being made about syphilis and the various ailments it causes. The other result of sex is pregnancy, as witnessed not only by Juliet's pregnancy, but the child that Lucio has fathered with Kate Keepdown. Given the negative consequences of sex, Isabella's decision to retreat to a convent may be understandable. As James Trombetta says in his article 'Versions of dying in *Measure for Measure*', 'It is unsurprising that chastity should appear in this society with the urgency of self-preservation'. Another irony of the play is the relatively light treatment of the play's bawds as opposed to the mutual and committed relationship of Claudio and Juliet. As Trombetta states in the article above, Vienna has 'turned against fornication and anarchic lust, but what it punishes is parenthood'. Claudio describes how signs of their lust 'With character too gross is writ on Juliet' *(Act 1, Scene 2)*.

Audiences may be made uneasy by the issue of consent. There is, of course, Angelo's attempt to force himself upon Isabella in exchange for Claudio's life, which Claudio thinks may be a bargain worth making. But there is also Mariana's tricking Angelo, which, some could argue, is also sex without consent. To a modern audience, Juliet has consented to be with Claudio, which makes the crime difficult to understand, but the same audience would be less easy with Mariana's deception of Angelo. A Shakespearean audience might focus more on the difference between a crime (fornication) and consummation (a stage in marriage). In this view, Mariana has simply completed a stage of her marriage with Angelo.

Unusually for Shakespeare, there are no portrayals of parents and children. Instead there are brothers and sisters: Claudio and Isabella, and Mariana and her brother who perished in a shipwreck. Escalus, in Act 2, Scene 1, says that the father of Claudio and Isabella was 'most noble', but otherwise the characters are unanchored by parental guidance. This adds to the insecurity of the matrimonial arrangements of both Claudio and Juliet, and Angelo and Mariana, which are paused or halted due to difficulties in arranging the dowries. The Duke is also unwed, though Lucio claims to the disguised friar that the Duke was 'a woodman' (Act 4, Scene 3), or a womanizer. His sudden desire to marry Isabella may be a sign of his renewed commitment to serve Vienna and to provide an heir. It is evidence of the lust that Isabella seems to inspire or the recognition of having met a woman who is a match for his intellect and morality, as his declaration in Act 3 would suggest: 'The hand that hath made you fair hath made you good' (Act 3, Scene 1). For her part, Isabella expresses no desire for marriage but, as Benedick (another late convert to marriage) exclaims in *Much Ado About Nothing*, 'The world must be peopled' (Act 2, Scene 3). The Duke concludes his proposal with an unromantic 'What's mine is yours, and what is yours is mine' (Act 5, Scene 1), suggesting that she could not turn down a marriage so financially advantageous to her. However, in the 2006 Complicite/National Theatre production, the Duke said 'what is yours is mine' with a sinister tone, suggesting that having escaped one predator in Angelo, Isabella would now have to submit to another.

Key quotation

The hand that hath made you fair hath made you good: the goodness that is cheap in beauty makes beauty brief in goodness; but grace, being the soul of your complexion, shall keep the body of it ever fair.
(Duke, Act 3, Scene 1)

Use a table like the one below to compare the relationships of Claudio and Juliet, and Angelo and Mariana.

	Claudio and Juliet	Angelo and Mariana
Agreement to marry	true contract *(Claudio, Act 1, Scene 2* fast my wife *(Claudio, Act 1, Scene 2)*	
Financial arrangement	we came not to / Only for propagation of a dower *(Claudio, Act 1, Scene 2)*	
Signs of love and affection		
Ending of the play		

Religion

The influence of religion in the play is apparent from the biblical source of its title, to the role of the Friar in the play's final act. But mixed with the religious is the opposite, the secular, in the very worldly concerns of the law, economics and sex. In Act 1, Scene 2, Shakespeare presents religious discussions juxtaposed with jokes about sexually transmitted diseases, a combination that to some could seem blasphemous, disrespecting religion. The Gentlemen and Lucio discuss the biblical commandments, **'Thou conclud'st like the sanctimonious pirate that went to sea with the ten commandments'** *(Act 1, Scene 2)*, noting that they may have forgotten **'Thou shalt not steal'** *(Act 1, Scene 2)*. They also discuss **'grace'**, which is a prayer said at mealtimes but also means 'the mercy and love of God', shortly before the arrival of Mistress Overdone *(Act 1, Scene 2)*, to whom they address puns about venereal diseases. It is into this scene that Claudio and the pregnant Juliet enter to be punished for **'our offence by weight / The words of heaven'** *(Act 1, Scene 2)*. In the world of Vienna, religion sits uneasily alongside the ribald underworld.

Religious orders play an important role in the play. The Duke disguises himself as a friar and Isabella is in the early stages of taking her vows as a nun. Make a bullet point list of references to these religious roles in the play and then write a paragraph explaining the use of religious orders in the plot of *Measure for Measure*.

Death

 The structure of the action in *Measure for Measure* derives from the rhythm of natural mutability [changeability] as it is experienced in human life. The pivotal events in the plot tend to be organic and physical: someone is pregnant, someone is sexually aroused, someone dies. The moral problems grow from the significance which Viennese society attaches to these events, and they are dissolved rather than solved in the comic conclusion.

(James Trombetta, 'Versions of Dying in *Measure for Measure*')

When Pompey the bawd is apprenticed to Abhorson, the humane Provost can see little difference between them; but there is a difference, and an important one. Together the pimp and the hangman stand for the two meanings in the pun *dying*: the executioner cuts off the life of his victim, and the pimp gets his customer to pay a little each time.

(James Trombetta, 'Versions of Dying in *Measure for Measure*')

The beginning of a new life, represented by Juliet's pregnancy, brings with it a condemnation of death for Claudio. The spectre of death hangs over the play, whether it is Claudio's genuine fear of it as expressed in Act 3, Scene 1 – 'Ay, but to die and go we know not where' – or Isabella's belief in an afterlife: 'Better it were a brother died at once, / Than that a sister by redeeming him / Should die for ever' *(Act 2, Scene 4)*.

The spectre of death hangs over the play

Activity 6

Throughout the play, Claudio expresses different feelings about his impending execution. Complete the spider diagram below with analysis of these different attitudes.

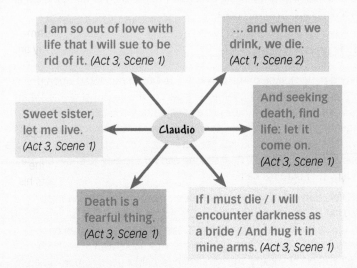

Writing about themes

Writing about themes requires you to show *how* Shakespeare presents them throughout the play, which he does in many different ways. To help you to revise themes in preparation for this, try the following activities:

- Make a table recording the key points of development of each theme.

- Consider how context, for example, contemporary attitudes towards authority or gender, might influence your understanding of the themes.

- Memorize key quotations that provide examples of themes.

- Analyse the language used to make a theme vivid, for example, the metaphors for the law or the puns about sex.

- Consider what Shakespeare may have been wishing to convey to the Jacobean audience about a particular theme.

- Connect your understanding of themes with your insight into Shakespeare's stagecraft, such as the structure of the play or characterization, that is, the juxtaposition of scenes showing different elements of justice or the characterization of the different figures representing aspects of justice, including Abhorson, the Provost, Escalus, Angelo and the Duke.

When writing about plays, it is important to consider different ways the text has been interpreted in various productions. *Measure for Measure* is a play that has been performed for over four centuries, being constantly reimagined to meet the concerns of the theatre makers and the audiences.

First performances

The first recorded performance of the play is on 26 December 1604, when it was performed at court before King James I as part of the seasonal revels. When performances were held at court, they were usually staged in a large hall – in this case, the banqueting hall at Whitehall – for a specially invited aristocratic audience. King James was the patron of the King's Men and it is likely that this was a chance for the company to flatter the new English king and for the king to show off the talented company that bore his name.

However, it is likely that the play had already been performed in the spring or summer of 1604 at the Globe Theatre where the atmosphere would be very different from at court. Unlike the banqueting hall, the Globe Theatre was a large open-air theatre. Performances would take place in the afternoon, with the audience representing all aspects of society. The 'groundlings' paid a penny (approximately the cost of a loaf of bread) to stand in the pit, the lowest area of the theatre near the stage. The aristocrats would sit in the 'Lords Rooms', which were expensive seats in the balconies towards the back of the stage. When Shakespeare was writing, he would be aware that his play would need to appeal to this wide audience and it is easy to imagine that the scenes with Elbow and Pompey were written to appeal to the groundlings, while the discourses on justice and authority may have been aimed at those in the expensive seats.

The actors of the King's Men would perform the roles. There are no existing cast lists for *Measure for Measure* so scholars need to surmise who played the roles, judging on past roles they played with the company, as actors tended to play similar types of role. Richard Burbage was the leading man at this time, so would either have played Angelo or the Duke. Robert Armin was the leading comic actor or 'clown'. He specialized in witty comic characters who pointed out the absurdity of the world around them, so may have portrayed Pompey. Women were not allowed on stage, so all the women's roles would have been played by boys in the company.

The plays were designed to be played straight through, moving fluently from scene to scene with only simple props or furniture, such as benches or stools, brought on to indicate a change of setting.

At the Globe, all performances were performed in daylight with no additional lighting. Music was important for establishing atmosphere. There was a musicians' gallery at the back of the stage and Shakespeare often specifically incorporated music into his plays, such as the melancholy song at the beginning of Act 4 of *Measure for Measure*. It is believed that at this time plays, even tragedies, usually ended with the actors performing a dance or a 'jig' on stage.

Costumes were an important aspect of theatrical productions in Shakespeare's time and audiences would be attuned to assessing a character's social status by the colours and fabrics of their costumes. Sumptuary laws dictated what was worn by different social groups to prevent people pretending to have a status or wealth they did not possess. Actors performing on stage were exempt from this and often wore clothes given to them by aristocrats or clothes specially made to depict the rank of the characters. Shakespeare's audience would expect to see the status of the characters reflected by their costumes. However, in *Measure for Measure*, the Duke discards his high status clothing for the robes of a lowly friar. The boy actors who were playing the women's roles would have worn women's clothing, with wigs and make-up adding to the illusion.

Activity 1

Make a note of when specific costumes or costume changes are suggested in the text. Consider what costume choices might have been made in Shakespeare's time and what choices a modern designer might make.

17th- to 19th-century productions

Although believed to have been popular when it was first written, *Measure for Measure* has fallen in and out of favour over time. During the Restoration period (1660–88), when the first women appeared on stage, there were adapted productions of the play, one of which removed the underworld characters and added music by Purcell. By 1720, Shakespeare's version began to be performed again. Sarah Siddons, the famous 18th-century Shakespearean actress, played Isabella in 1783 to great acclaim. Some illustrations from the time show her dressed in dark veils, with a heavy crucifix around her neck, kneeling with an arm outstretched in supplication. Her intense performance in Act 3, Scene 1, in which she examined her brother for any signs of reluctance to avoid her shame, was particularly admired.

However, in the Victorian age, the play fell out of favour, with many objecting to its apparent lack of morality. The Victorian writer Coleridge said that it was the 'only painful' work Shakespeare wrote. He found it 'disgusting' and 'horrible', noting in particular Angelo's 'degrading' behaviour towards the women in the play.

20th-century productions

At the beginning of the 20th century, there was a residual reluctance to stage the play. The actor Simon Callow writes that the play was rarely revived 'on the grounds of both structural weakness and scandalous morality'. It was also not considered a very rewarding play for the actors, with neither the Duke nor Angelo having the dramatic appeal of Hamlet or Othello. However, Tyrone Guthrie's 1933 production of the play at the Old Vic, with Charles Laughton as Angelo and Flora Robson as Isabella, was considered a success by many and began a fresh examination of the play's importance. Laughton's performance portrayed Angelo's tortured and brooding depths.

Engraved for the Lady's Magazine.

Mrs SIDDONS, in the Character of Isabella, in Measure for Measure, by Shakespere.

Sarah Siddons' dramatic performance proved popular with 18th-century audiences

Activity 2

a) Read the following views about Laughton's performance:

> As it happens, however, Angelo's utterances are so tortured and tortuous the line – and the **syntax** – is so broken up by emotion and mental twistings and turnings, that it is sometimes hardly verse at all.
>
> (Simon Callow, *Charles Laughton, A Difficult Actor*)

> John Armstrong's costume for him turns Laughton into a terrible black bird [...] while his features are full of dark malignant horror: 'When the actor shows us Angelo in the scene where he bargains with Isabella, brooding over the girl like a lustful black bat, he gives a glimpse of such murky depths in the man's nature that we no longer despise him for his sins. Instead we admire him that he fought his temptations so long.' This account – by W.A. Darlington in the *Daily Telegraph* – is a masterly description of the Laughton effect.
>
> (Simon Callow, *Charles Laughton, A Difficult Actor*)

b) Discuss what you learn about Laughton's interpretation of Angelo from these comments and whether or not it agrees with your understanding of the character.

syntax the structure and organization of sentences

After the Second World War, *Measure for Measure* was performed more frequently, with Peter Brook's 1950 production starring John Gielgud making a particularly strong impression. This production was remarkable for showing Brook's ideas of how the 'Holy and Rough' of the play co-exist, accepting the play's contradictions and surprising juxtapositions rather than eliminating them. It combined the 'holy' rituals of characters like the Duke with the 'rough' satiric energy of the underworld characters.

In 1976, a young Meryl Streep played Isabella in a 'Public Theater Shakespeare in the Park' production. Dressed in a white nun's habit, Streep presented Isabella's 'chaste, cold intelligence' while also suggesting the character's 'natural warmth' opposite a thin, black-clad 'malevolent' John Cazale as Angelo.

A very different approach was taken by Michael Rudman, whose 1981 National Theatre production was set on a mythical Caribbean island, with most of the roles played by black actors. Rudman's setting was foreign enough for the audience to imagine that the events of the play could believably occur in a location that was both distant and familiar, perhaps resonant of Fidel Castro's Cuba. Norman Beaton played Angelo opposite Yvette Harris's Isabella. The production was praised for its exuberant handling of the underworld scenes, the liveliness of its public scenes and its unashamedly joyous interpretation of the ending.

The striking poster advertising the 1976 production starring Meryl Streep

> ### Activity 3
>
> Discuss what political and social events of the 20th and early 21st centuries might have increased interest in the play *Measure for Measure*.

21st-century productions

In 2004 (revived in 2006), Simon McBurney directed a strikingly visual production of the play at the National Theatre, in collaboration with his company Complicite. McBurney highlighted the nightmarish aspects of the play with his use of shadowy lighting and stylized movements. This **non-naturalistic,** updated production explored the theme of surveillance, as live video feeds projected images of key scenes.

Naomi Frederick's cropped haired Isabella was dressed plainly in a drab novice habit and flat shoes, her beauty hidden, while Angelo wore a smart suit, suitable for a successful executive or politician. The prisoners were costumed in orange jumpsuits like those in American prisons and images of George W. Bush, the American president at the time, were projected on screens, emphasizing the play's political relevance.

Also in 2004, the Shakespeare's Globe Theatre production was set in the Jacobean period and performed as an uncomplicated comedy with period dances linking the first three acts and ending the play. In this production, Isabella (Sophie Thompson) and the Duke (Mark Rylance) were united in their innocence and shocked by the evil that surrounded them. There was much broad humour, with the Duke hiding in a laundry basket full of women's underwear at one point, limping with a thorn in his foot at another and fainting at the sight of blood from Ragozine's head.

Michael Attenborough's 2010 updated production at the Almeida Theatre explored the contemporary relevance of the play. The underworld scenes seemed to be inspired by London's Soho with their neon signs and dancing girls. Rory Kinnear's Angelo transformed from a modest, awkward, bespectacled middle manager to a sweating predator. Anna Maxwell Martin, dressed plainly in black, matched Kinnear's intensity when refusing his offer. One reviewer felt that the two were so clearly mirror images of each other in their absolute beliefs that they formed a more natural union than that between Isabella and the Duke.

In 2015, Cheek by Jowl, in partnership with Moscow's Pushkin Theatre, also focused on the theme of abuse of power in their production performed in Russian with English subtitles. In one scene, Claudio wore a sign around his neck proclaiming his guilt, surrounded by cruel uniformed officers, while ominous red containers dominated the set. Dominic Cavendish, in the *Daily Telegraph*, said the production tapped 'the play's sense of a governmental experiment gone hideously awry'.

The Young Vic's updated 2015 version directed by Joe Hill-Gibbins highlighted two key themes of the play: religion and sex. Angelo carried a Bible, Isabella was dressed modestly as a nun and characters were seen in prayer, while, in contrast, there were also projections of Claudio and Juliet having sex and a room filled with blow-up sex dolls. The set design combined both religious and sexual imagery, with one reviewer noting that it resembled both a 15th-century painting of the Last Supper and a sex shop.

non-naturalistic stylized, not realistic or life-like

Tips for assessment

Upgrade

Remember that demonstrating an understanding of different productions of *Measure for Measure* is a way of reflecting on different interpretations and context.

Michael Rudman's production ended the play with celebration

Alternative productions

One of the most radical reworkings of *Measure for Measure* was Charles Marowitz's production staged at the Open Space Theatre in 1975. Marowitz cut and reallocated lines to emphasize the cruelty of the play. Discarding Shakespeare's convenient substitutions of Mariana for Isabella or Ragozine's head for Claudio's, in this production, Angelo strips Isabella and then rapes her. When she returns to the stage, she discovers her brother's severed head. Marowitz introduced a new character, a Bishop, who at the play's end denies Isabella justice and instead covers up the crimes of those in power.

In 2002, NT Education, in collaboration with the London Bubble Theatre, produced an interactive production. The actors spoke to the audience, involving them in the action and moving them around the space. The audience was encouraged to assist with sound effects, such as the noises in the prison, and were invited to think about the play's concepts. At one point, for example, a sign was held up that read 'Is this person true to themselves?' A red carpet as well as a large desk and a variety of flags were used to signify the status of the Duke. The casting was gender blind, with women playing some roles typically performed by men, such as Escalus. Pompey read a list of prisoners to be executed, which was updated to include contemporary politicians, the winner of *Pop Idol* and 'the cab driver who brought me here'.

Richard Wagner's opera *Das Liebesverbot* (*The Ban on Love*), premiered in 1836, was based loosely on *Measure for Measure*. The action is moved to Palermo with the Angelo character being changed to Friedrich, a German outsider. A recent production by Teatro Real was performed on a brightly coloured stage with contemporary touches like a 'smartphone duet' in the Claudio/Isabella scene.

Activity 4

a) The ending of the play is seen as problematic by many and has been interpreted in many different ways. Read the descriptions of how the ending was performed in various productions and make notes about the different ways the relationship between the Duke and Isabella is presented at the end.

- At the end of the 2004 Complicite/National Theatre production, the newly joined pairs are scattered around the stage. Mariana and Angelo kneel on opposite ends of the stage with their heads bowed. When the Duke announces **'What's mine is yours'** he takes a long pause before saying to Isabella, in a dominating way, **'and what is yours is *mine*'**. Isabella looks blankly out at the audience.

Activity 4 continued

- In the 2002 London Bubble/National Theatre production, the Duke impulsively says **'Give me your hand'** to Isabella but she barely registers it, as she is still responding to the wonder that Claudio is alive. The Duke reacts with annoyance at himself – why did he choose the wrong time to ask her? Isabella hugs Claudio when the Duke is speaking to the others. More hesitantly, the Duke approaches her. Claudio begins to take Isabella away with him, but Isabella stops and looks at the Duke. The play ends with them holding their glances – ambiguous, but seeming to suggest she may be at least intrigued by him.

- In the 2010 Almeida production, Isabella greets the Duke's proposal with a stunned silence as if in total disbelief that, after everything she has gone through, this unwanted marriage was to be the final outcome.

- The 1983 Michael Rudman/National Theatre production has an uncomplicatedly happy ending. Isabella accepts the Duke's offer joyously and without hesitation. A carnival atmosphere envelops the last minutes of the play.

b) Write a paragraph explaining the different ways the Duke's proposal at the end of the play could be interpreted.

Writing about performance

When writing about performance, consider how:

- particular casting or actor's choices can influence your understanding of a character

- key moments can be interpreted by different designers, actors or directors

- the play may be relocated to different settings other than those specified by Shakespeare

- radical re-interpretations of the script may include updating the time period or altering the gender of characters and can bring advantages and disadvantages

- the script may be edited or re-ordered

- performance choices may be shaped by the interests and concerns of the audience.

Academics and critics analyse works of literature from various perspectives. For example, they may study the work to uncover attitudes towards gender, politics or language. They may debate previous assertions about the text or the conventions of its genre. Awareness of different critical opinions can help you to demonstrate your understanding of different readers' and audience's opinions, and how a piece of literature is open to interpretation. This chapter covers just a few of the critical stances from which *Measure for Measure* could be analysed.

Political or Marxist criticism

Marxist literary criticism takes its inspiration from the writings of socialist philosophers Karl Marx (1818–83) and Friedrich Engels (1820–95), and analyses texts by identifying class wars, power struggles, economics and oppression. Marxist criticism might consider:

- **capitalism** versus **socialism**
- the roles of the **proletariat** and the ruling class
- shifts in power and dominance
- how money, property and goods are exchanged.

One way Shakespeare explores social class is by having the Duke discard the outward signs of wealth to assume the guise of a poor friar. In this disguise he is able to move freely among the proletarian characters, such as the jailers and underworld characters, as well as hearing the confessions of upper-class characters like Claudio. It could be argued that the corrupted state of the working class is due to the unfair distribution of wealth in Vienna. Escalus, an establishment figure, feels Claudio should be treated more leniently because of his noble father and is kinder to Froth, who has some inherited wealth, than he is to Pompey, who does not appear to have the same advantages of birth. The working-class characters, like Pompey, are shown scrabbling to make a living, changing from one disreputable profession to another in order to survive. Elbow has taken a job for which he is ill-suited 'for some piece of money' *(Act 2, Scene 1)*. Mistress Overdone could be seen as an example of the evils of capitalism, as she makes money from the vices of her clients. After the Duke experiences the underworld, he does not seek to make changes in the distribution of wealth, but instead returns to the status quo. He once again takes on the rights and privileges of the ruling class and imposes his will upon others.

> **Key quotation**
>
> 'Your friar is now your prince...'
> *(Duke, Act 5, Scene 1)*

The Young Vic production used technology such as projections, in this instance showing the characters of Pompey and Froth

capitalism a political system that encourages private trade and industry for profit

proletariat a collective term for working-class people

socialism a political system that promotes state ownership of industry and aims to empower the working class

A rich source for Marxist criticism is the various marriage contracts in the play, where a woman must provide a suitable dowry or marriage portion in order to complete the marriage contract.

> The meaning of sexual relations is transformed, though not beyond recognition: the Duke's vision of marriage, expressed when he usurps the hand of Isabel, is of a strict economic exchange: 'What's mine is yours, and what is yours is mine.'
>
> (James Trombetta, 'Versions of Dying in *Measure for Measure*')

The proletariat characters Mistress Overdone and Pompey in a 2015 performance at The Globe, London

Activity 1

a) Read the quotations below about the various economic arrangements between the couples in the play and explain how Trombetta's suggestion that financial exchange is associated with marriage is supported.

> **This we came not to**
> **Only for propagation of a dower**
> **Remaining in the coffer of her friends** *(Claudio, Act 1, Scene 2)*

> **her brother Frederick was wrecked at sea, having in that perished vessel the dowry of his sister.** *(Duke, Act 3, Scene 1)*

> **which was broke off,**
> **Partly for that her promised proportions**
> **Came short of composition** *(Angelo, Act 5, Scene 1)*

> **We do instate and widow you with all**
> **To buy you a better husband.** *(Duke, Act 5, Scene 1)*

b) 'The women in the play are particular victims of the economic system of Vienna.' Write a paragraph explaining how far you agree with this statement and your reasons why.

Christian literary criticism

Christian literary criticism examines texts for religious influences. Christian criticism might include:

- Christian symbols or iconography, such as crosses, lambs or doves
- biblical references
- study of characters' attitudes towards God and spirituality
- attitudes towards the afterlife
- depictions of prayers
- comparisons with the life and beliefs of Jesus
- characters who are members of religious orders.

Many critics feel that Christianity infuses the play. The critic G. Wilson Knight contributed an influential Christian reading of the text. In his view, the Duke performs a Christ-like role and he asserts that *Measure for Measure* is best understood when read as a **parable** (see the quotation on page 95).

> The play must be read, not as a picture of normal human affairs, but as a parable, like the parables of Jesus. The plot is, in fact, an inversion of one of those parables – that of the Unmerciful Servant (Matthew xviii); and the universal and level forgiveness at the end, where all alike meet pardon, is one with the forgiveness of the Parable of the Two Debtors (Luke vii) [...] And if ever the thought at first sight seems strange, or the action unreasonable, it will be ever found to reflect the sublime strangeness and unreason of Jesus' teaching.
>
> (G. Wilson Knight, *Measure for Measure* and the Gospels', Casebook Series, *Shakespeare's Measure for Measure: A Selection of Critical Essays*)

parable a simple story that contains a moral or spiritual lesson

The parable of the Unmerciful Servant teaches the lesson of a servant who has his debt forgiven but refuses to forgive someone who owes him. The comparison could be made with Angelo, who is discovered to have sinned while refusing to forgive those who have sinned before him. The parable of the Two Debtors has the message that those who have sinned the most but then repent are forgiven and most loved by Christ. This too would point to the surprising act of the Duke's forgiveness of Angelo given his many transgressions. This reading of the play turns Angelo, a greatly disliked figure by many, into a person worthy of forgiveness and redemption. These ideas are reinforced by the play's title taken from Matthew 7: 1–2 in the Bible.

Another rich area for Christian literary criticism is the characters' attitudes towards death and the afterlife. Isabella feels less anguish about Claudio's death because of her Christian belief in an afterlife, whereas Claudio has doubts. She is certain that Claudio will be Angelo's 'swift ambassador' 'to heaven' *(Act 3, Scene 1)* whereas Claudio fears to go 'we know not where' *(Act 3, Scene 1)*. Rather than seeking heaven in death, he declares that 'The weariest and most loathed worldly life' is 'paradise / To what we fear of death' *(Act 3, Scene 1)*. Angelo, on the other hand, perhaps in a return to his previous strict Christian beliefs, welcomes rather than fears death and his last words in the play are to declare, 'I crave death' and 'I do entreat it' *(Act 5, Scene 1)*, perhaps hoping to find a comfort in death that has evaded him in life. The Duke's last speeches contain a series of pardons and absolutions, not to prepare the characters for death, however, but for marriage.

Activity 2

Read the scenes between the Duke and Juliet in Act 2, Scene 3 and between Claudio and the Duke in Act 3, Scene 1, when the Duke, disguised as a friar, is offering religious guidance. Make bullet point notes about how religion, repentance and death are portrayed in these scenes.

Feminist criticism

Influenced by the **feminist** movement and the impulse to re-evaluate women's role in society, feminist critics often focus on:

- strong or transgressive female characters, who break boundaries, rules, social order or moral codes
- examples of women's place within the **patriarchy**
- representations of women's bodies and biology
- reconsideration of assumptions about the roles women play
- examining and challenging the language used to describe femininity and female roles
- comparing the contextual expectation of characters with those of the present day.

A feminist critic may offer an alternative reading of a text in which a female character has been misread, judged or stereotyped. They may also identify female characters who seem to break the bounds of what would be expected of a woman at the time the text was written. Isabella is a character who has invited this type of re-examination.

> **feminist** someone who supports the equality of men and women
>
> **patriarchy** a society ruled by men

 Another aspect of her character that ought to be particularly appealing to a twenty-first century audience is that what is sexy about Isabella is her intelligence. Although Lucio calls her *pretty Isabella*, not much is made of her beauty. What strikes us is the astonishing way in which she can hold her own in debate. Entering a convent in the early seventeenth century was one of the few ways an upper class girl could avoid the marriage market and the perils of child-bearing. It might offer a woman her only chance of a life of study, contemplation, intellectual development. A feminist reading of the play might see Isabella helping Mariana to outwit the men and end up with exactly what Mariana wants – even if we do not quite understand why she wants it.

(E.D.M. Woodhouse, English Association Shakespeare Bookmarks Number 2)

Aside from Isabella, there are women who are depicted as victims of the patriarchy, such as Juliet and Mariana, whose marriage hopes flounder while waiting for male relations to provide a dowry, or those who live off the demands of the patriarchy, such as Mistress Overdone. Juliet and Mistress Overdone are both characters defined by their biology: Juliet by her pregnancy and Mistress Overdone for her role in spreading sexually transmitted diseases.

There are also female characters, mentioned but never seen, who are victimized by men.

> The women whose stories create the play's narrative strands are joined by others: Kate Keepdown the sex worker, deceived and abandoned by Lucio (3.2.192–97); Bridget, the once-mentioned mistress of Pompey (3.2.76); and Mistress Elbow, the Constable's pregnant wife who has been sexually harassed by Froth, the rich young man about town. These women are shadowy figures, but their stories extend the play's social world in which sexual relations seem peculiarly unmanageable even when the women conform to respectable social expectations.
>
> (Kathleen E. McLuskie, 'Gender in *Measure for Measure*', British Library)

Most of the female characters, except for those in religious orders, are explicitly sexually available to the male characters. As an apprentice nun, Isabella occupies a grey area where her sexual availability is still to be decided. Some critics believe that Claudio sends his sister to plead his case knowing that Angelo will find her attractive. It is also a matter of debate to what extent she willingly consents to marriage to the Duke or if she is being forced into it by a powerful man.

Activity 3

Some modern critics argue that although Isabella could be seen as a victim of sexual harassment, her subsequent actions show her supporting rather than challenging the patriarchy. Write a paragraph explaining whether or not you agree with this, supporting your opinion with evidence from the text and reference to the critical opinions above and on page 96.

Structuralism

Structuralism is a type of literary criticism that analyses the narrative structure and seeks to uncover patterns. A key concept of structuralism is binary opposition, which seeks to identify the dichotomies and conflicts between different groups or concepts. For example, in *Measure for Measure*, some binary oppositions include:

- male/female
- rich/poor
- false/true
- lust/chastity
- heaven/hell
- liberty/imprisonment
- wisdom/foolishness

Structuralists would look at the patterns in the text, for example, when Angelo's lust is put in opposition to Isabella's strict chastity or the Duke's transformation from wealth to poverty.

Key quotation

Some rise by sin and some by virtue fall,
Some run from breaks of ice and answer none,
And some condemned for a fault alone. *(Escalus, Act 2, Scene 1)*

Activity 4

The language of the play reflects the extreme opposition of ideas. In the table below are examples of oppositions and contrasts. Copy and complete the table, explaining Shakespeare's use of oppositions and the effects achieved.

Oppositions	Explanation
too much liberty... / Turns to restraint *(Claudio, Act 1, Scene 2)*	At this point, Claudio has been arrested for having acted freely with Juliet. He is going to be imprisoned, but could also have acted with more 'restraint' in his relations with Juliet. He suggests that there are often consequences for too much freedom: 'when we drink, we die'.
I would tell what 'twere to be a judge / And what a prisoner *(Isabella, Act 2, Scene 2)*	
The law hath not been dead, though it hath slept... / Now 'tis awake *(Angelo, Act 2, Scene 2)*	
Never could the strumpet... / but this virtuous maid *(Angelo, Act 2, Scene 2)*	
I had rather give my body than my soul. *(Isabella, Act 2, Scene 4)*	
I have been an unlawful bawd... / yet I will be content to be a lawful hangman *(Pompey, Act 4, Scene 2)*	

neurotic illness an illness caused by mental instability or anxiety

repression not allowing the expression of powerful thoughts or impulses

Psychological literary criticism

Some critics have been influenced by the psychoanalytical writings of Sigmund Freud (1856–1939) and more recent psychological theories. They seek to use the language and concepts of analysis in literary criticism. Some areas of interest include:

- hidden or subconscious meanings
- analysis of symbols and what they say about the characters' psychological state
- family dynamics
- the behaviour of characters that can be explained by psychological concepts such as obsession, neurosis, narcissism and repression
- how the biography of the author might influence the text.

Freud explored how the 'id' which was the source of a person's basic drives, such as their 'libido' or sexual impulses, was often in conflict with the rules of society and moral expectations. Repressing these sexual needs could, he believed, lead to **neurotic illness**. One interpretation of Angelo is that as the result of years of sexual **repression**, he experiences a mental breakdown, leading to his violent and highly sexual actions.

Activity 5

Read this student's attempt at offering a psychological reading of Angelo and then add at least three sentences to complete it, providing evidence from the play.

Other characters describe Angelo as a character who denies any emotion, with the Duke claiming that he 'scarce confesses / That his blood flows' and Lucio confirms that his blood is 'snow-broth' or cold. The repression of his desires may lead to his erratic behaviour when he meets Isabella. Unable to find a healthy outlet for his sexual needs, he attempts to take Isabella by emotional coercion by saying he would pardon her brother in exchange for her virginity. However he seems confused by his attraction to her, questioning his very identity – 'What dost thou and what art thou, Angelo?' – as his actions are so much in conflict with his sense of identity. By Act 4, Scene 5, his guilt leads to a breakdown, indicated by his fractured soliloquy.

Freud also identified the Madonna-whore complex in which some men divide all women into 'Madonnas', that is those who are pure, as exemplified by Mary the mother of Jesus, and 'whores' or sexually promiscuous women, as exemplified by Mary Magdalene, the prostitute depicted in the New Testament. Men with this complex are said to love women they identify as Madonnas, but desire women they label as whores.

That Angelo divides women in this way is suggested by his treatment of Juliet, who he dismisses as a 'fornicatress' *(Act 2, Scene 2)* but seconds later is willing to meet Isabella, who is described as a 'virtuous maid' *(Act 2, Scene 2)*. In his soliloquy after the meeting with Isabella, he declares that 'Never could the strumpet [...] stir' him as 'this virtuous maid', Isabella, has *(Act 2, Scene 2)*. So while he divides women into these two over-simplified groups, his sexual desires are more complex. Isabella's virginity and lack of availability adds to her appeal. However, after taking

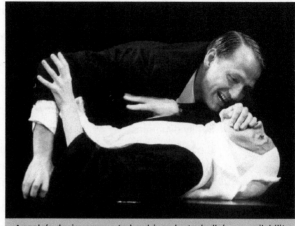

Angelo's desire seems to be driven by Isabella's unavailability

her virginity, as he believes, Angelo appears to be finished with Isabella and orders the execution of her brother, which would certainly end any prospect of a future relationship with her, as she is no longer a 'Madonna'. His expectation of purity in women is also asserted when he claims that Mariana's 'reputation was disvalued' as one of his reasons for refusing to marry her *(Act 5, Scene 1)*. His attitude to women seems paradoxical; he only wants to possess a woman who is unobtainable.

Reader response criticism

Reader response criticism highlights the interaction between a reader and a text. It considers the creative input of the reader/audience in the creation of a work of art. These critics look for:

- active responses from audiences/readers
- occasions when different audiences/readers may respond differently to a text
- fluctuations in the audience's/reader's response, such as shifting sympathy
- the actual experience of the reader/audience when reading/seeing the text.

Measure for Measure is a play that can be looked at from many perspectives and, given the interests and concerns of the audience, may be received in many different ways. An audience with an interest in strong, intellectual female characters might view Isabella as a heroine, refusing to bow to the outrageous demands of those around her, while others might view her unsympathetically as someone who puts her lofty ideals above the life of her brother. Audience members might find that their sympathy for Isabella wavers from scene to scene. An audience that is aware of political repression might react with alarm and recognition at Angelo's cruel punishments, while those interested in psychological study may view him as a man in the grip of insanity and therefore worthy of sympathy.

Another aspect of reader responses are the creative interpretations of the directors, designers and actors who all have individual interactions with the play and contribute to how it is received by an audience.

Activity 6

Consider your own reaction as a reader of *Measure for Measure* and try to analyse your own response by answering the following questions.

a) Did your sympathy for the characters shift as you read the play?

b) When you first read the text were you making certain predictions that did or did not come true?

c) Do you think the gender of the reader affects how they receive the text?

d) Did you respond differently to the text when you saw it in performance rather than reading it?

e) Do you believe a 21st-century audience receives the text differently from one in Jacobean times?

Writing about critical views

To improve your writing about different critical responses to the text, try the following:

- Read critical opinions that are contradictory, weigh them up and decide which you most agree with and why.
- Choose a scene and analyse it from different critical perspectives. You might choose a scene such as Act 2, Scene 2 and analyse it from feminist, psychological, Christian and/or political perspectives.
- Consider what is known about the characters' mental states and how that could enrich a psychological reading of the text.
- Reflect on the characters' attitudes towards money and power, and how that could influence a Marxist reading of the text.
- If you are quoting a critic, make sure you acknowledge them.
- Don't take credit for ideas that aren't yours, but do build on and interact with other writers' ideas.
- Remember you do not have to agree entirely with a critic. It is important you understand different viewpoints but develop your own ideas.

A key to exam success is practice. Take advantage of any opportunities to study past papers and undertake timed writing. Many students find the demands of writing under tight time constraints challenging, but this gets easier with training.

Understanding the question

When you get an exam question, read the question carefully. Underline key words and phrases to ensure that you steer your response in the correct direction. Some questions may be extract-based, directing you to provide a close study of a particular section of the text, while others will be focused on character, theme, genre or context. No matter what the question, you will need to demonstrate that you can express yourself clearly and make relevant points about language, structure and form.

Character-based questions

'Isabella and Angelo have more in common than any other characters in the play.' To what extent do you agree with this statement?

The focus of this question is on the similarities and differences of the characters of Isabella and Angelo. Both are articulate characters with rigid points of view. However, you may identify differences in their attitudes towards sex, religion and justice. Remember that 'to what extent' means that you do not have to agree or disagree totally with the original statement – you are weighing up the evidence and coming to a conclusion.

Theme-based questions

'Punishment and mercy, two sides of justice, are shown to be illogical and inconsistent in the Duke's Vienna.' Explore this statement in light of your choice of scenes from the play.

The question requires you to display your understanding of several concepts: how the theme of justice is portrayed in the play, the different displays of punishment and mercy, and how to connect these to the way the Duke rules Vienna. There are many relevant scenes from the play that you could choose to discuss. Some key moments that you might consider include: Act 1, Scene 3, when the Duke discusses laws with the Friar; Act 2, Scene 1, the comic legal case with Elbow and Pompey; and Act 5, Scene 1, when the Duke delivers both mercy and punishments.

Context-based questions

> 'Measure for Measure reflects the anxieties of the Jacobean age.' Analyse the play with reference to how it portrays the interests and concerns of the time.

You must select specific aspects of the play that reflect the anxieties of the time in which it was written, such as religion, rulers and disease. Some lines of inquiry might include the play's relevance to James I, the portrayal of Catholicism and the role of women at this time. However, make sure that your analysis is not just historic, but also literary. Remember to consider how understanding the context underpins your insight into the play's characters and themes.

Genre-based questions

> How does Shakespeare use the conventions of comedy to deliver the unsettling themes of Measure for Measure?

To answer this question well, you must analyse the conventions of Shakespearean comedy, such as the use of disguise, wordplay, clown figures and an ending resulting in multiple marriages. This question provides the opportunity to discuss different interpretations of the play's genre and how key scenes, like the play's ending, may be performed as a comedy or as something darker.

Extract-based questions

> Looking closely at Act 1, Scene 2, from Claudio's line, 'Fellow, why dost thou show me thus to th'world?' to Claudio's line, 'With character too gross is writ on Juliet,' analyse the portrayal of desire and marriage in the play. Consider how Shakespeare uses language to explore these themes.

An advantage of an extract question is that you do not have to spend time choosing what section of the play you are going to discuss and you have the text before you, enabling you to provide detailed language analysis. In this extract, you might look at the negative portrayals of desire ('a thirsty evil', 'lechery') and contrast these with the more positive depictions of his relationship with Juliet ('fast my wife', 'mutual entertainment').

Planning your answer

Given time constraints, it is tempting to rush into writing your answer without making a plan. However, a common feature of successful answers is evidence of planning. Plans help you to organize your ideas and make sure that you don't leave out important points.

There is not one 'right' way of making a plan, but some techniques include bullet point lists, spider diagrams and paragraph plans. Below is a sample question with two different plans in response.

> 'The prison is the ultimate symbol of Vienna.' To what extent do you agree with this statement in relation to *Measure for Measure*?

Activity 1

Using the spider diagram below, add additional ideas and specific quotations to support key points.

Spider diagram

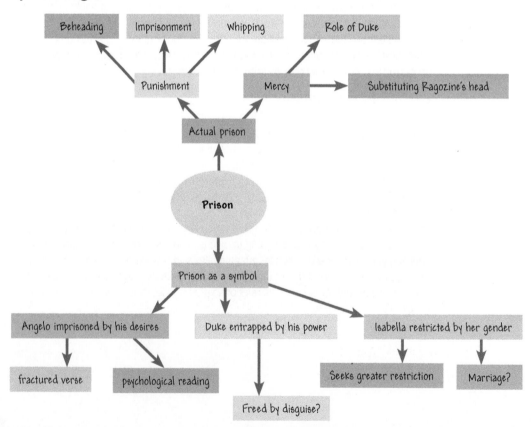

Tips for assessment

When using lists or diagrams as a planning method, consider numbering your ideas so that you work through them in an effective order. Put a tick next to a point as you make it, so you avoid making it twice or leaving it out altogether.

Paragraph plan

Introduction Walled city of Vienna allows for the juxtaposition of court and underworld characters, highlighting similarities and contrasts. The prison shows the best and worst of characters imprisoned.

Paragraph 1 Contrast Claudio and Barnardine – both prisoners but with very different moral codes. What do we learn about Vienna by their treatment in the play?

Paragraph 2 Order versus chaos: How is order imposed in Vienna and in the prison? How do anarchic characters like Pompey escape punishment?

Paragraph 3 Marxist reading of the play: characters imprisoned by the status quo. Characters forced to break the law or perform other distasteful duties for economic gain. Marriage as a form of imprisonment.

Paragraph 4 Characters imprisoned by their desires: analysis of Mariana and Angelo with particular note on language.

Conclusion The play's tension between those who try to impose order and the anarchic desires of characters like Angelo, Barnardine or Pompey. Play's comic resolution is attempt to restore order.

Activity 2

Experiment with these different methods of planning by creating two different styles of plan for the following question:

'Typically passive women characters are idealized in literature.' Discuss this statement in relation to the character of Mariana in *Measure for Measure*.

Tips for assessment

It is important to make a plan, but remember that it should be done quickly. Write in note form, not full paragraphs.

Writing your answer

Structuring your response

Although there are no set rules about how to structure your answer, some students find it helpful to think of their response using a template like this:

Introduction: Opening argument

Paragraph 1: at least three points with supporting examples and analysis

Paragraph 2: at least three points with supporting examples and analysis

Paragraph 3: at least three points with supporting examples and analysis

Conclusion: bring points together and arrive at a final conclusion.

When practising your answers, guidance like this can be helpful as it reminds you to support your ideas with evidence and analysis, but it can also be restricting. For example, you may wish to write more than five paragraphs or you may have a wide-ranging series of points you wish to make, so don't feel bound by this. However, using a template for revision and planning practice can increase your confidence in your ability to structure a response quickly.

Tips for assessment

Use some of the wording of the question in your first paragraph and subsequent paragraphs as this will help to keep you on topic and reassure the examiner that you have understood the focus of the question.

Prioritizing your ideas

A common error in essay-writing is to make all points sound equally important, which lessens the sense of a well-shaped, balanced and thoughtful argument. In order to avoid this, try to use **discourse markers** to guide the reader through your response. Examples include the following words and phrases:

- To introduce order: first; in the beginning; next; subsequently; finally.
- To prioritize or emphasize: most important; significantly; notably; especially.
- To suggest comparisons or contrasts: alternatively; on the other hand; in contrast; similarly; in the same way; equally.

discourse marker 'signpost' words or phrases that help to direct the reader to the order, importance or relationship of ideas being presented

Activity 3

Write a paragraph contrasting the characters of the Duke and Angelo using at least three discourse markers to clarify your ideas.

Developing an academic writing style

Below is an example of a student's writing, which demonstrates some difficulties in assuming an academic register:

Examiner's comments

Too great a use of 'I.' A response should not just rely on personal opinion.

Vocabulary is too informal: 'really ridiculous', 'hardly a crime!'

It may not seem like it, but the play is in 'modern English' and saying it wasn't 'easy to understand' could suggest a lack of effort.

It is useful to point out a source of 'conflict' but this point needs to be developed.

> I think the laws in Vienna are really ridiculous. It seems like some people get away with a lot, while others, like Claudio, are arrested when what they have done is hardly a crime! I didn't like the scene where the two Gentlemen were talking with Lucio because I think they were making jokes but they weren't ones that are funny or even easy to understand. It would be so much easier if this was written in modern English. However, it did get more exciting when Claudio was brought onstage. That is when the injustices of Vienna were clear and you could see there was going to be some conflict. I think Claudio is my favourite character.

Except for one 'however', drawing attention to one point, all other ideas are given equal weight; there is no ordering or prioritizing.

Saying that Claudio is their favourite character is a random assertion with no evidence to support it.

Activity 4

Read an examiner's comments on the piece of writing above and then rewrite the paragraph with the improvements suggested.

Using quotations

Important to your success is your ability to select and analyse quotations from the play in order to support your argument. Ideally, your examples should be brief and embedded in a grammatically correct way into your writing.

For example:

> Escalus's name suits him well as he frequently shows that he represents the well-balanced scales of justice. He quickly realizes that Pompey is 'a tedious fool' (Act 2, Scene 1) whereas he treats Elbow more kindly: 'it hath been great pains to you' (Act 2, Scene 1). The humanity of his reactions contrasts with those of the 'strict' Angelo, who presents himself as 'Justice' personified while breaking laws himself.

Activity 5

The student below wants to analyse Lucio's role, but has struggled with embedding short quotations. Read the response and then rewrite it so that the quotations are shorter, presented more correctly and clearly analysed.

Lucio can be an irreverent character. For example, he greets Isabella by saying,

'Hail virgin, if you be – as those cheek-roses

Proclaim you are no less – can you so stead me

As bring me to the sight of Isabella' (Act I, Scene 4)

He is also a good friend as he pleads with Isabella to help her brother: 'Unless you have the grace by your fair prayer / To soften Angelo' (Act I, Scene 4). In Act 2, Scene 2, he acts like her coach, urging her to continue her debate with Angelo: 'Give't not o'er so: to him again, entreat him, / Kneel down before him, hang upon his gown'.

Tips for assessment

Not all your quotations in your response need to be long. An analysis of a well-chosen word is worth more than longer, unanalysed quotations.

Citing critics and other readers' opinions

You may wish to refer to the opinions of others in your essay. It is important that you make it clear when words are not your own. For example, you might write:

The critic David Daniell offers a critical interpretation of the Duke, accusing him of being a 'disreputable' leader who 'slid' from his responsibilities by assuming the role of a 'meddling false friar'.

If you do not have a critic that you specifically want to quote or cite, you can instead evaluate a general critical position or adopt a critical stance yourself. For example:

A feminist reading of Isabella would highlight her unwillingness to submit to the typical roles available to women of the time and instead plan to devote her life to study and contemplation.

Activity 6

a) Memorize a few key quotations from reviews of the play and academic articles.

b) Choose a question and write a paragraph adopting a critical stance using the quotations you have memorized.

Sample questions

Below are examples of some of the different styles of questions that you might be asked in the exam, with some of the typical wording. Notice that one type of question is to make a statement and then ask if you agree with it. In those instances you do not need to agree whole-heartedly with the statement, but you should find and analyse evidence that either supports or disagrees with it. Other questions might direct you to a particular scene or excerpt or focus on a theme or character. In all instances, you will be required to write in a fluent, knowledgeable way about the play and show that you can analyse the relevant sections of the play using correct literary terminology.

1

'Angelo is both the hero and the villain of the play.' How far do you agree with this statement?

2

Starting your discussion with a detailed analysis of the beginning of Act 4, Scene 1, discuss the portrayal of love in the play.

3

'Comedy and tragedy are evenly balanced in *Measure for Measure*.' In light of this comment, analyse the elements of comedy and tragedy in the play.

4

How does *Measure for Measure* reflect the limited roles for women in early 17th-century England?

5

Examine the role of Pompey in the play and discuss how Shakespeare uses his character to reveal the play's themes and concerns.

6

Referring closely to Act 2, Scene 4, how does Shakespeare present the exploitation of power in the play?

Sample answers

Sample answer 1

'What dost thou or what art thou, Angelo?' Analyse the presentation of Angelo in the play with relation to the play's key themes.

Despite his name, which sounds angelic, Angelo is not a very nice character. At first, characters like the Duke and Escalus think he will do a good job running Vienna because he is cold-blooded and 'strict'. He pretends to be reluctant to take power (he says he needs more of a 'test' before receiving this honour) but, very shortly after the Duke leaves, he orders that the bawdy houses are torn down and he has Claudio and Juliet arrested. It seems particularly unfair that Claudio is arrested. After all, compared to the actions of others, like Mistress Overdone, he doesn't seem very guilty and he is willing to marry Juliet, who says their love is 'mutual'.

> Angelo isn't 'very nice' is irrelevant, better to connect him to the play's themes.

> Uses a short quotation, but doesn't analyse it; just retells the plot.

However, Angelo shows that he is guilty of the same faults as Claudio when he discovers his lust for Isabella. In Act 2, Scene 2, he falls in love with Isabella despite knowing that she is training to be a nun. This shows that he is as guilty of desire as other characters and desire is one of the play's themes. However Angelo's desire is a twisted, secret thing as he pretends to be one thing on the outside but is something else inside. We can see this because he tries to hide his real nature from other characters.

> Finally mentions one of the play's themes.

> This is a missed opportunity to use some quotations to support points.

Jacobean England was a Christian country and there were rules about marriage and sex. Angelo is one of many characters acting in a way that could be considered inappropriate for a Christian. Angelo does have a conscience though and in his soliloquies he can be seen battling with himself, which might make the audience more sympathetic to him at times.

> Attempts to include some context, but needs to develop more.

Once Angelo's downfall begins, it gets worse and worse. Not only does he force himself upon a woman he assumes is Isabella, he also lies to Isabella and unfairly orders her brother Claudio to be beheaded. Some productions highlight his mental instability in Act 4, with one production going so far as showing Angelo self-harming during the 'Good night' soliloquy.

> Good to mention an interpretation of the scene, but could connect more to question.

Uses a quotation, but it would be useful to analyse it.

Another theme in which Angelo plays a part is justice. Escalus complains that Angelo thinks he is 'Justice' so cannot be reasoned with. However, his justice is shown to be unfair and cruel – as the title of the play suggests he should treat others as he would be treated himself and he is guilty of the sins that he accuses others of committing.

Death is another theme that relates to Angelo because he threatens others with death but is also facing death himself at the end of the play. It is only the pleading of Mariana and Isabella that saves him in the end. Mariana is a character who is treated very badly by Angelo, but she seems to have a weakness for bad men, as she says they are better for being 'a little bad'. However, most productions don't make this seem like a very happy match and it is hard to think they will have a joyous marriage. But at least she does help him escape death. She shows more mercy towards him than he does towards Claudio.

A well-chosen quotation, but it needs more analysis and connection to question.

These points might have worked well in the first introductory paragraph.

So although Angelo does not have the largest role in the play, he is probably one of the most interesting and complex characters. Shakespeare shows him to be a man who does not know himself and who is a victim of his own ambitions and desires. It is hard to feel happy that he is married to Mariana, who he has treated badly and does not seem to love, but a play ending with his death, might have been too sad, particularly for a play that is meant to be a comedy.

The opening sentence lacks formality ('very nice') and an academic register, which does not bode well. However, the student shows some understanding of the play and uses some effective brief quotations. Useful points are made about connections to themes like desire, death and justice but these are not well-developed. There is little evidence of literary terminology or analysis of language. More awareness of genre and critical opinions would improve this response.

Sample answer 2

> 'In *Measure for Measure*, the "sinners" are presently as sympathetically as the "saints".' How far and in what ways do you agree with this statement?

The very title of the play suggests that we are all sinners who will be judged according to our actions by referencing the biblical quote 'with what measure ye mete, it shall be measured to you again' (Matthew 7: 2). In the play it is difficult to divide the characters into 'sinners' and 'saints'. It is tempting to align characters such as the Duke and Isabella on the side of the saints and Angelo and Claudio as sinners, but an examination of the various characters shows that this basic dichotomy may not be so clear.

Demonstrates a subtle understanding of the question and its challenges.

In the Vienna of the play, which clearly mirrors aspects of Jacobean London, there are the sinful underworld characters, such as Pompey and Mistress Overdone, who contrast with the more 'saint-like' characters of the Duke and Isabella, who, for added emphasis are both depicted assuming the dress of religious orders. One of the fascinating structural features of the play is the juxtaposition of the court scenes and convent/friary scenes with those of the bawdy streets and prisons. Yet instead of highlighting the differences between these worlds, characters like Angelo, Claudio and Lucio show that some characters may straddle both and that sinners exist in the underworld and the court.

Discusses structure with some insight.

Returns confidently to the question.

Act 1, Scene 2 provides an example of language that combines both religious and sexual elements. Using a range of puns and sexual innuendo, Lucio and the two Gentlemen discuss 'the ten commandments' and 'grace' while also joking about the 'many diseases' that might be contracted under Mistress Overdone's roof. This is a comic portrayal of sinners, encouraging the audience to laugh at the excesses of Mistress Overdone and her customers.

Discusses language using the correct terminology.

However, a more sympathetic portrayal of sinners occurs later in the same scene, when Claudio and Juliet are arrested and led out into the street to be shamed. Shaming those accused of fornication was common in Jacobean England and some productions emphasize this shame by having the characters wear signs around their necks, such as 'Fornicatress'. Claudio is an excellent example of a 'sinner' who is treated sympathetically in the play. Although he has technically broken the law of the land, the act was for their 'mutual entertainment' and it is only the accident of

Analyses context and one possible interpretation from a production.

Uses short, well-chosen quotations and shows an understanding of possible audience reactions.

Juliet's pregnancy that caused them to be caught. Throughout the play, Claudio expresses remorse. In Act 3, Scene 1, he announces to the Duke, who is disguised as a friar, that he is 'prepared to die'. However when a chance for his salvation comes, if his sister would 'yield' her 'virginity' to Angelo, his all-too-human desire to stay alive is likely to be greeted more sympathetically by a modern audience than his 'saint-like' sister's refusal.

Appropriate discussion of different readers' interpretations and well-chosen quotation.

Both Isabella and Angelo could be said to be characters who initially present themselves as 'saints'. However the rigidity of their positions can make them unappealing to modern audiences. One 20th-century critic described Isabella as a 'prig' and her unbending rejection to save her brother's life is sometimes met with gasps when she proclaims in Act 2, Scene 4, 'More than our brother is our chastity'. Angelo's facade of sainthood is quickly revealed to be false and his many sinful actions are further complicated by the audience's awareness that he is also a hypocrite.

Discusses a named critic's point of view and offers alternative points of view.

The 20th-century critic G. Wilson Knight provides a Christian reading of the text in which the Duke serves an almost Christ-like role as he teaches the citizens of Vienna through a series of tests and dialogues. However, many contemporary productions of the play reject this interpretation, finding something ominous in this Duke of 'dark corners', who assumes disguises in order to spy on others. It may be left to the largely silent female characters of Mariana and Juliet to demonstrate the humble, patient suffering associated with Christianity.

In conclusion, it is not easy to decide which characters are most worthy of our sympathy and which can simply be labelled 'sinner' or 'saint'. Shakespeare seems to admit the difficulty of delivering justice fairly in the play's final act. Even the most disreputable of characters, Barnardine, who neither expresses contrition nor seeks mercy, is pardoned along with the other characters. This leaves only the complaining Lucio, a character who the audience may have enjoyed and sympathized with, to bear the harshest of punishments.

This answer begins confidently with an appropriate analysis of the play's title. A nuanced discussion of 'saints' and 'sinners' follows with a number of clear references to the audience's sympathy and different interpretations. There are some well-chosen scenes and quotations, though a little more language/genre analysis would have been welcomed. The student has the confidence to interact with critical opinions and to introduce appropriate context.

Sample answer 3

'Although she only speaks in one scene, Juliet serves as an important example of the role of women in Jacobean England.' Starting with a discussion of Act 2, Scene 3, explain to what extent you agree with this statement.

Some critics believe that, at one stage, Juliet's role was a larger one. Unusually, although she appears in three scenes (Act 1, Scene 2; Act 2, Scene 3; and Act 5, Scene 1), it is only in Act 2, Scene 3 that the audience hears her speak. Some critics view her as an example of a typical woman silenced by a patriarchal society and punished for her biology, that is, her ability to give birth. In Jacobean England, she serves as a reminder of the limited choices for women, who were often reliant on a dowry as part of a marriage contract and who are powerless in relation to those who would humiliate or exploit them.

> Offers what could be interpreted as a feminist reading of the character.

> Appropriate use of context, which informs response to the question.

In Act 1, Scene 2, Claudio and she are arrested, though productions vary in whether or not they choose to show her at this point. Some emphasize her vulnerable pregnant state, while others omit her from the scene altogether, instead focusing on Claudio's words and his struggle with imprisonment. Claudio's account makes clear the complications and difficulties with marriage contracts in Jacobean times. Although he considers her 'fast my wife', the evidence that they had sex before 'outward order' was established, that is before being married, is shown in her pregnancy, which is 'writ on Juliet'. Their wedding was delayed as they were waiting for 'a dower' – a similar problem to Mariana, whose dowry was lost at sea with her brother.

> Considers different interpretations in production.

> Well-chosen, brief quotations to support the answer.

Isabella provides a contrast with Juliet, as she has decided to join a religious order and forego the company of men, but she expresses affection for Juliet, calling her 'cousin' and saying that she does this in 'apt affection'. Even the judgemental Isabella offers a matter-of-fact 'O, let him marry her' as a response to Juliet's dilemma, unaware at this point of Angelo's strict new regime. The characters of Isabella and Juliet are further contrasted when Angelo, in Act 2, Scene 2, dismisses Juliet with

> There is still no mention of the key scene that was meant to 'start' discussion.

Offers a psychological reading.

only 'needful' care, while he allows Isabella, who the Provost describes as a 'very virtuous maid' to enter. A psychological reading of this might suggest that Angelo suffers from a Madonna/whore complex, where he divides women into one of two incompatible groups, yet does not apply a similar judgement to his own compromised actions.

Finally begins analysis of the named scene.

In Act 2, Scene 3, when Juliet's voice is finally heard, it is in a difficult scene with the Duke, who pretends to be attending to her spiritual needs while she is in prison. Although a Jacobean audience may have found the suffering to which Juliet is subjected in this scene as necessary for her eventual salvation, a modern audience may recoil at its cruelty. The Duke tells her that her 'sin' is of 'a heavier kind' than Claudio's, suggesting that although their relationship was mutual, the burden of remaining chaste was hers to bear. She humbly repents and confesses, but is given little comfort in the Duke's response, which can be viewed as cruel, as he announces Claudio 'must die tomorrow', an act he could easily stop by throwing off his disguise and resuming authority.

Comments on the structure and genre of the play.

At the end of the play, when, as expected in a Shakespearean comedy, the characters are going to be sorted into married pairs, Mariana is asked if she is 'married', 'a maid' or 'a widow', with Lucio offering a fourth possibility, 'a punk' or a whore. These four categories define Jacobean women. By her marriage to Claudio, Juliet is allowed to move from the category of 'punk' (or 'fornicatress') to 'married'. However, this redemption only happens after she suffers, including her repentance and her belief that her lover has been killed. In some productions, only Claudio and Juliet are portrayed as a happy couple, while others suggest that all the couples are happy or all are shattered by what they have experienced. The relative silence of the women at the play's end, when the Duke dictates all the other characters' fates, highlights their lack of power.

The student starts boldly, offering a feminist reading of the character of Juliet and showing a clear understanding of Juliet's importance in the play. There is an impressive grasp of different critical readings of the play and how various productions have interpreted key scenes. However, the question does ask for Act 2, Scene 3 to be the starting point and more analysis of this scene would have provided opportunities for discussing language features. Overall, this is a wide-ranging response demonstrating a depth of understanding, but more focus on the key scene is needed.

Sample answer 4

Explore Shakespeare's examination of death in *Measure for Measure*. Remember to include contextual information and how the text may be interpreted by different readers.

For a comedy, death shadows 'Measure for Measure' to a surprising degree. Not only are there the obvious plot points about the beheadings or potential beheadings of various characters, but images of disease and absence recur throughout. This sits uneasily with the supposedly happy ending of the play, in which it is down to the Duke's whim if a character is killed or married. There is also the irony of Angelo apparently preferring death to his marriage to Mariana; 'I crave death more willingly than mercy'.

This is a promising opening making a number of points concisely.

Death has a strong impact in Act 4, Scene 2, when it is treated comically in the scene between Pompey and Abhorson and seriously in the scene between the Duke and the Provost. Abhorson and the Provost have a comic dialogue when Abhorson's job of cutting off men's heads is described as 'a mystery'. While this word means a trade that has to be learnt, it could also refer to the mystery to what happens to someone after death. Pompey puns on Abhorson's job by referring to him having 'a hanging look', which means looking sad, but also is another form of execution. The reality of Abhorson's job is brought home when the Provost tells him to 'provide your block and axe'. This links to the two men awaiting execution: Claudio and Barnardine.

A well-chosen scene for discussion.

Appropriate analysis of language.

Claudio is portrayed as a good man who has sinned and who has a reasonable fear of death. Barnardine is a perpetual criminal who has sinned but doesn't care if he lives or dies. The contrast in their attitudes towards death is clear from their dialogue. In Act 3, Scene 1, Claudio announces 'Death is a fearful thing' and explains how, when we die, we 'go we know not where'. His desperation to live drives him to beg his sister to intervene on his behalf, much to her disgust. By Act 4, Scene 2, he seems sadly resigned to his fate.

Uses some well-chosen quotations though analysis could be more insightful.

In contrast, Barnardine is either asleep or drunk and unwilling to take the matter seriously. Even when he is pardoned at the play's end, he seems unchanged and unmoved by the experience.

A short, under-developed paragraph. Needs to link more to question.

Gives relevant context.

Sex and death are connected in the play. In Act 1, Scene 2, characters discuss the venereal diseases (for which there were no effective or reliable cures in Jacobean times) that characters catch from Mistress Overdone's establishment. Shortly before the play was believed to have been written, another disease, the plague, spread across London, killing thousands. Therefore the fragility of life would be apparent to Shakespeare and his audiences. Claudio is facing death because of his relations with Juliet. Angelo immediately orders the beheading of Claudio after having relations with Mariana (believing it is Isabella). Although there was capital punishment in Shakespeare's time, this was not the punishment for fornication, but Shakespeare is taking dramatic license (and relocating his play to Vienna) to explore this extreme situation.

Makes a good attempt to bring in other interpretations, but struggles to connect to the question.

Some productions emphasize Angelo's relationship with death. For example, Charles Laughton played him dressed in a costume that some critics said made him look like 'a black bat'. John Cazale also wore black, contrasting with the virginal white of Meryl Streep's Isabella. Black is a colour associated with death. In the 2004/2006 National Theatre/ Complicite productions, Angelo was stained with the blood of Ragozine's head and seemed at times to be suicidal himself.

Mariana is also a character that can be associated with death. The death of her brother at sea, causing the subsequent loss of his fortune, has left her almost entombed in her 'moated grange', cut off from signs of life in a sort of living death.

Includes some appropriate ideas but final paragraphs feel rushed and under-developed.

A sense of mortality may explain the actions of the Duke as well. He is unmarried and apparently childless, which means that he has no obvious heir. His surprising proposal to Isabella in the final minutes of the play may be due to his desire to bring life rather than death to Vienna.

Although this student makes many useful points, this is a good example of a response that would be improved by a few minutes of planning. At present the ideas don't necessarily link and build, making it difficult to follow a sustained argument. However, there is a clear understanding of the play, some brief, well-chosen quotations, some correct contextual information and some evidence of different interpretations of the play.

Glossary

ad-lib unscripted words, said without preparation

allegory a story where characters represent moral or political ideas

alliteration the repetition of the initial sound or letter of words

anaphora the repetition of key phrases at the beginning of a line or sentence to create a dramatic effect

antithesis placing a statement and an opposing statement in the same sentence

aside brief lines spoken by actors and addressed to the audience rather than the other characters on stage

blank verse unrhymed lines of poetry with a regular metre

caesura a pause or break near the middle of a line of verse

capitalism a political system that encourages private trade and industry for profit

comedy a play that ends happily for most of the characters and often focuses on amusing characters or incidents

coup de theatre a dramatic effect notable for its suddenness or element of surprise

Deus ex machina a surprising and unlikely plot device that brings about a resolution to what seemed to be an impossible situation

dialogue conversation between two or more characters

discourse marker 'signpost' words or phrases that help to direct the reader to the order, importance or relationship of ideas being presented

dramatic irony when the audience knows something one or more characters on stage do not

elided merged

euphemism an indirect or more positive way of expressing something unpleasant or harsh

extended metaphor when a metaphoric comparison continues for a few lines or sentences

feminist someone who supports the equality of men and women

foregrounded brought to prominence/to the attention of the audience

gallows humour humour expressed in a bleak or desperate situation

genre a category or style of literature or art

hybrid genre a work of literature or art that combines elements of two or more different genres

iambic pentameter lines of verse consisting of five feet (iambs), each consisting of one unstressed and one stressed syllable

irony words that express the opposite of what is meant; the difference between what may be expected and what actually occurs

malapropism using an incorrect word for another, often creating a comic effect

metaphor a figure of speech applied to something to suggest a resemblance, without using the words 'like' or 'as'

meta-theatrical theatre that draws attention to its own artifice, e.g. by pointing out that it is a play rather than reality

misogynist a person who dislikes or is prejudiced against women

neurotic illness an illness caused by mental instability or anxiety

non-naturalistic stylized, not realistic or life-like